Developmental Psychology and Early Childhood Education

Developmental Psychology and Early Childhood Education

A Guide for Students and Practitioners

DAVID WHITEBREAD

Los Angeles | London | New Delhi
Singapore | Washington DC

© David Whitebread, 2012

First published 2012

Apart from any fair dealing for the purposes of research or private study,
or criticism or review, as permitted under the Copyright, Designs and
Patents Act 1988, this publication may be reproduced, stored or
transmitted in any form, or by any means, only with the prior
permission in writing of the publishers, or in the case of reprographic
reproduction, in accordance with the terms of licences issued by the
Copyright Licensing Agency. Enquiries concerning reproduction outside
those terms should be sent to the publishers.

SAGE Publications Ltd
1 Oliver's Yard
55 City Road
London EC1Y 1SP

SAGE Publications Inc.
2455 Teller Road
Thousand Oaks, California 91320

SAGE Publications India Pvt Ltd
B 1/I 1 Mohan Cooperative Industrial Area
Mathura Road
New Delhi 110 044

SAGE Publications Asia-Pacific Pte Ltd
33 Pekin Street #02-01
Far East Square
Singapore 048763

Library of Congress Control Number: 2011925514

British Library Cataloguing in Publication data

A catalogue record for this book is available from the British Library

ISBN 978-1-4129-4712-1
ISBN 978-1-4129-4713-8 (pbk)

Typeset by C&M Digitals (P) Ltd, Chennai, India
Printed in India at Replika Press Pvt Ltd
Printed on paper from sustainable resources

This book is dedicated to my wife Linda, the love of my life, and to my two gorgeous daughters, Lizzie and Sarah, without whom I would have written this much quicker. But it wouldn't have been nearly as much fun!

Contents

Acknowledgements

This book is the culmination of a lot of reading, thinking, talking, listening and teaching over many years, and I am indebted to the innumerable young children, early years educators and developmental psychologists whose paths I have crossed for their many and varied invaluable contributions to this inevitably long and tortuous process. In particular, I want to thank the young 5–6-year-old children who were in my class in 1980–81, who consistently demonstrated metacognitive and self-regulatory abilities they were not supposed to have, according to the research I was being introduced to on Monday afternoons within my MEd.

I am also indebted to early years colleagues in schools, to the Early Years and Primary PGCE teaching team, and the Psychology and Education Academic Group in the Faculty of Education at Cambridge, all of whom have provided a wonderfully stimulating environment for me to test out my ideas over the years. And, finally, I must say a huge thank you to my many wonderful students, on the Early Years PGCE, the MPhil and MEd Psychology and Education course, and on the PhD programme. It has been a huge privilege, over the years, to work with such brilliant and committed young people who care so passionately about young children and their education.

The publisher and author would also like to thank the following:

Taylor & Francis for:

'High/Scope evaluation at 27 years', Schweinhart and Welkart (1993) in K. Sylva and J. Wiltshire (1993) 'The impact of early learning on children's later development: a review prepared for the RSA inquiry "Start Right"', *European Early Childhood Education Research Journal*, 1, 17–40.

'Multistore model of memory (based on Atkinson and Shiffrin 1968)' from Whitebread, D. (2000) *The Psychology of Teaching and Learning in the Primary School*.

'How children learn: The constructivist model' from Whitebread, D. (2000) *The Psychology of Teaching and Learning in the Primary School*.

'Piaget's number conservation problem', from Whitebread, D. and Coltman, P., (eds) (2008) *Teaching and Learning in the Early Years*, 3rd edn.

Harlow Primate Laboratory for:

Image of baby monkey feeding and holding cloth mother.

Wiley-Blackwell for:

'Explanation of Ainsworth's Strange Situation Technique', Cowie, H. (1995) from Barnes, P. (ed.) (1995) *Personal, Social and Emotional Development of Children*.

'Profile of vocabulary growth typical of children in their second year' from Plunkett, K. (2000) Development in a connectionist framework: rethinking the nature–nurture debate', from Lee, K. (ed.) *Childhood Cognitive Development: The Essential Readings*.

'Vygotsky's "zone of proximal development"' in Smith, P.K. and Cowie, H. (1991) *Understanding Children's Development*.

'Bruner's nine glass problem' from Bruner, J.S. (ed.) (1966) *Studies in Cognitive Growth*.

American Association of the Advancement of Science for:

'Learning through imitation', Meltzoff, A.N. and Moore, M.K. (1977) Imitation of facial and manual gesture by human neonates. *Science*, 198.

BBC for:

Brain size and social group, David Attenborough, *Life of Mammals*.

HarperCollins for:

'Hughes's hiding game', Donaldson, M. (1986) *Children's Minds*.

McGraw-Hill for:

'Different types of play in schools', Moyles, J. (1989) *Just Playing? The Role and Status of Play in Early Childhood Education*.

Little Acorns to Mighty Oaks for:

Elinor Goldschmeid's *Treasure Basket*, www.littleacornstomightyoaks.co.uk

Allen D. Bragdon Publishers, Inc for:

'Your brain and what it does', www.brainwaves.com

Every effort has been made to trace all copyright holders, but if any have been overlooked, or if any additional information can be given, the publishers will be pleased to make the neccessary amendments at the first opportunity.

About the Author

David Whitebread is a Senior Lecturer in Psychology and Early Years Education in the Faculty of Education, University of Cambridge, and currently Convenor of the Psychology and Education Academic Group. He gained a degree in Psychology and English Literature from Keele University in 1970 followed by a Primary PGCE (infants) at Clifton College in Nottingham, where his tutor was Dorothy Gardner (nee Glynn) from whom he claims direct handshaking rights from Susan Isaacs. He began his teaching career with a hugely enjoyable 12 years as an early years teacher, in Leicestershire and at the British School in Tehran (from where he and his wife returned on the fall of the Shah in 1979). Having undertaken an MEd at Nottingham University, and started a part-time PhD concerned with children's cognitive development, under the supervision of the renowned Piagetian scholar Eric Lunzer, he went on to gain a lecturer post at Homerton College, Cambridge in 1986. In 1990, he instigated the revival of the Early Years PGCE at Homerton, and was Director of the Early Years and Primary PGCE course in 1997–2002. When the college merged with the university, he established a highly successful Masters course in Psychology and Education within the newly established Faculty of Education, and now is mostly engaged in research and supervision of PhD students.

He has conducted a number of research projects, principally concerned with the development of metacognitive abilities in young children and the role of play in early learning. He has published numerous book chapters and academic journal articles on these topics, and presented papers and given keynote speeches at various national and international conferences. His publications include *The*

Psychology of Teaching and Learning in the Primary School (2000) and *Teaching and Learning in the Early Years* (3rd edn, 2008). As an expert in early years education and children's early psychological development, in 2009 he appeared on a BBC *Horizon* programme concerned with early years education and on a BBC Science programme examining the educational claims made by toy manufacturers. He is a national executive member of TACTYC, the professional association of early years educators, and has been a governor at Homerton Nursery school (now Children's Centre) in Cambridge for many years. Recently, he was appointed as a consultant expert at the LEGO Learning Institute in Denmark.

David is married to Linda, and has two lovely daughters, all of whom are currently doing their bit to save the planet.

List of Figures

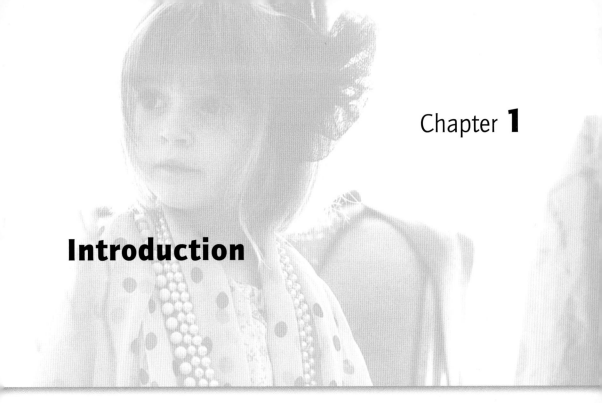

Chapter **1**

Introduction

Child Development and Early Years Education

This is a particularly exciting time to be writing this book. To begin with, and perhaps most fundamentally, it is an exciting time to be involved in early years education. For many years, the education of our youngest children has been a neglected and massively under-funded cottage industry, made up mostly of enthusiastic amateurs working in largely voluntary or very poorly paid capacities and working in church halls, scout huts and the like. Suddenly, and perhaps too suddenly in some ways, not only in the UK, but internationally, in the developed world, the developing world, and increasingly even in the least well-developed countries in the world, early years education is being taken seriously and is enjoying unprecedented levels of investment and development. The sheer speed of these developments is currently presenting major challenges, but there can be no doubt that this new recognition is long overdue and enormously important. All of us involved in early years education at this time have an exciting opportunity to contribute very significantly to the transformation of this, the most important phase of a child's education, into a professional, evidence-based enterprise which can make a real difference to the quality of children's lives, and to the societies into which they grow up as citizens.

At the same time, there is equally exciting progress in developmental psychology. We are currently experiencing a massive leap forward in our understandings about young children's development which, as is often the case with scientific advance, is largely a consequence of new technologies. So, just as it is accepted in astronomy that Galileo's most important contribution was in his development of the telescope, rather than his ideas about the Earth travelling around the Sun, so in developmental psychology, the emergence of an array of new methodological tools has been of enormous benefit. As we shall see as we review the various kinds of evidence later in the book, these have included the use of video, of computers, of non-invasive neuroscientific methods, of techniques developed in evolutionary biology, and of a range of new research designs and methods of analysis. All of these technological and methodological advances have enabled us to increase enormously what we know and understand about young children. Most importantly, they have contributed to a revolution in developmental psychology. When I trained as a psychologist in the late 1960s and early 1970s, much of the research with young children was methodologically limited and tended towards a deficit model of the young child, focusing on what they could not do. By contrast, the more sophisticated approaches of modern developmental psychology have enabled researchers to uncover a wealth of information about all the astonishing early achievements of the young child.

So, to be writing a book at this time, which attempts to distil what we currently know from developmental psychology that might be helpful in our attempts to introduce young children to the world of education, is a delight and a challenge. It is a challenge because of the wealth of knowledge we now possess about young children's capabilities, but it is a delight because the book can focus so clearly on what children can do, rather than on their limitations.

Focusing on what children can do is, however, more than simply a pleasing, self-indulgent emotional response. It is actually enormously important in relation to early childhood education. As humans we have evolved, mostly in the Pliocene period when we lived for several million years as hunter-gatherers, to learn and develop in particular ways. These early adaptive processes have fashioned the human brain to be enormously efficient at processing information, but it achieves this in particular ways, which have made us astonishingly brilliant at some tasks (such as remembering faces, learning language, learning from one another), but rather poor at others (such as remembering names, understanding physics, working out how our latest gadget works by reading the manual). In the strange modern world in which we now find ourselves, we need to be aware of how our brain has evolved to learn and develop, so that we can build on our strengths as a species, rather than exposing our weaknesses. One of my earliest pieces of published writing about young children's learning concerned their learning of mathematics (Whitebread, 1995). In that chapter, I argued that understandings of how young children learn, derived from modern developmental research, showed us why traditional methods of teaching mathematics (abstract, removed from meaningful contexts, using conventional written symbols and taught algorithms) were likely to be generally ineffective and undermine children's confidence. With a better informed approach (practical, placed in meaningful contexts, building on children's own representations and strategies), we could harness the strengths of human learning and help children to become confident and able young mathematicians.

This book is an attempt to extend this kind of approach to the much broader sweep of children's development and learning.

Developing Children as 'Self-regulating' Learners

Indeed, the guiding principle and fundamental theme of the book is that young children can, with benefit to themselves as learners and developing individuals, do more for themselves than has previously been thought or commonly provided for in educational settings. They can take responsibility for their learning and ownership of it, and derive enormous benefit from doing so. They can become what is referred to in the developmental literature as 'self-regulating' learners. This is a theme which runs through each chapter of this book, as it relates as much to children's emotional and social development as it does to the development of their intellectual capacities. In the final chapter of the book, however, it is the central focus and works to bring together the principles and implications for pedagogy derived from the various aspects of children's development covered in the intervening chapters.

There is currently widespread interest and enthusiasm in the early years world for fostering self-regulating or 'independent' learning among young children, as attested by a number of publications (Featherstone and Bayley, 2001; Williams, 2003), by the current enthusiasm for such approaches as Reggio Emilia and High/Scope, both of which emphasise children's autonomy and ownership of their learning, and by recent official government guidelines. Recent initiatives, circulars and curriculum documents from various government agencies have offered a range of suggestions as to what independent or self-regulated learning might involve. In the revised QTS Standards entitled Qualifying to Teach (TDA, 2006), for example, teacher trainees are required under Standard S3.3.3 to:

> teach clearly structured lessons or sequences of work which interest and motivate pupils and which make learning objectives clear to pupils ... [and] promote active and independent learning that enables pupils to think for themselves, and to plan and manage their own learning.

In the Curriculum Guidance for the Foundation Stage (DfEE/QCA, 2000), which established the new curriculum for children between 3 and 5 years of age, one of the stated 'Principles for early years education' is that there should be:

> opportunities for children to engage in activities planned by adults and also those that they plan and initiate themselves. (p. 3)

Of course, as is often the case with these kinds of policy documents, these are simply statements of well-established good practice rather than anything startlingly new (despite the attempts of politicians to present them as such, with the implication that they personally have come up with a brilliant new idea that, somehow, has eluded the entire teaching profession). While a commitment to encouraging children to become independent or self-regulating learners is very common amongst early years teachers, however, at the level of everyday class-room realities, there are a number of problematic issues. The need to maintain an orderly classroom, combined with the pressures of time and resources, and teachers' perceptions of external expectations from headteachers, parents and government agencies, can often militate against the support of children's independence. This is unfortunate and often counter-productive. The kind of overly teacher-directed style this tends to engender may create an impression of having 'covered' the curriculum, but is largely ineffective in promoting learning in young children, and does not help at all in the larger project of developing children's ability and confidence to become independent learners.

I remember very vividly, for example, my own two children's experiences with pre-school groups. At one group they attended, which claimed to teach the children to read, write, etc. and which had quite a long waiting list, they were greeted at the door and directed to the table at which they should sit, where materials were already neatly arranged and ready for some pre-designed craft activity. Here, they were told not to touch anything until the adult helper took them through each stage of the process, often helpfully re-adjusting things that proved too difficult for them to achieve. After 20 minutes, all the children at the table had produced identical robots, Mother's Day cards or whatever and they moved on to the next table where another activity was already waiting for them. The children made few if any choices, were never required or encouraged to have their own ideas, and had an almost entirely seat-based experience. At the end of the morning, they rushed up to greet me (or my wife), and usually forgot to bring with them any of the perfect creations they had been rather peripherally involved in. At a second pre-school (well, at the time, it was actually called a playgroup), for which, ironically, there was much less parental demand (probably as no claims were made about the formal learning of literacy), the children arrived to find a whole array of possible play activities from which they could choose, including some seat-based craft-type activities, but also construction materials, sand and water trays, bikes and other vehicles, a dressing-up rail, a 'home' corner for imaginative play, and so on. At the end of the morning, they would rush up enthusiastically, usually dressed up as Princess Smartypants or Wonder Woman, to show us two bits of cornflake packet stuck together with sellotape which was their magic helicopter or new little puppet friend Margaret, and which had to be carefully held onto so they could finish it at home, and then they had to be persuaded to transform themselves back into children and leave so that the nice ladies could tidy everything away until tomorrow. You can probably tell by the way I have written about these two establishments where I thought our children were doing some real learning. It was in the playgroup, of course, where they were being properly challenged, where what they could do was being recognised and built upon, and where they were learning not only practical, cognitive and social skills, but also how to make choices, develop their own ideas, and manage and regulate their own learning.

On top of the current constraints and difficulties pushing early years practitioners away from play-based and towards more adult-directed and formal approaches, there is also, understandably, often a lack of clarity as to the nature of independent or self-regulating learning. It is clear from governmental policy statements, as I cited above, that there is currently a strong commitment to the area of independent learning. However, there is also confusion and a need for clear definition. To begin with, while on the one hand early years practitioners are being asked to provide 'personalised learning' and respond to the 'Every Child Matters' agenda, at the same time they are being continually bombarded by 'top-down' pressures to force-feed all their great variety of children with set curricula and formalised 'standards'. In some recent policy guidelines (such as the recent Early Years Foundation Stage [DfES, 2006] document) and commentaries, furthermore, the emphasis has unhelpfully shifted more towards helping children with personal independence skills and in becoming an independent *pupil*, i.e. being able to function in a classroom without being overly dependent on adult help. This is quite distinct, however, from the concern to help children develop as independent *learners*, i.e. being able to take control of, and responsibility for, their own learning. It is for this reason that the term 'self-regulation' is increasingly preferred, with its emphasis on the learner taking control and ownership of their own learning. As we shall see, it is also a term which has a strong tradition within the developmental psychological literature.

Over the last few years, I have worked with 32 Cambridgeshire early years teachers on the Cambridgeshire Independent Learning (C.Ind.Le) Project (Whitebread and Coltman, 2007; Whitebread et al., 2005). This research has established that young children in the 3–5 age range, given the opportunity, are capable of taking on considerable responsibility for their own learning and developing as self-regulated learners, and that their teachers, through high-quality pedagogical practices, can make a highly significant contribution in this area. (More detail about this research is provided in the final chapter of this book.) The findings which have been derived from the C.Ind.Le project, and other similar research, however, have been a large part of the inspiration to write this book, and permeate each chapter.

The Impact and Nature of Quality in Early Years Education

Developing the educational provision for our youngest children is, of course, of vital importance. It is now well established that a child's educational experience in the early years has both immediate effects upon their cognitive and social development and long-term effects upon their educational achievements and life prospects. Sylva and Wiltshire (1993) reviewed a range of evidence which supports this position. This evidence includes studies of the Head Start programmes in the USA, the Child Health and Education Study (CHES) of a birth cohort in Britain and Swedish research on the effects of day care.

To begin with, these various studies appeared to produce inconsistent findings. Early studies of the Head Start programmes, for example, which provided pre-school places for children in economically and socially disadvantaged areas in the USA, suggested immediate cognitive and social gains, but little lasting effect. The CHES study, on the other hand, found a clear association between pre-school attendance and educational achievements at age 10. More recent analysis, however, has revealed that lasting long-term effects are dependent upon the quality of the early educational experience. Sylva and Wiltshire (1993) noted particularly the evidence of long-term impact achieved by High/Scope and other high-quality, cognitively orientated pre-school programmes. The most famous of these programmes was the Perry Pre-school Project in Ypsilanti, Michigan, directed by David Weikart, which was part of the Head Start initiative and later developed into what is now known as the High/Scope programme. Figure 1.1 presents some of the results from a follow-up study he conducted with a colleague with a cohort of 65 children who had attended this half-day educational programme over two years during the mid-1960s. Their outcomes at age 27 were compared to a control group of children from the same neighbourhood who had not attended the pre-school programme. As we can see, as well as achieving significantly better high school grades, the children who had attended the pre-school programme had been arrested on significantly fewer occasions, had higher earnings, had needed to receive less support from social services, and were much more likely to own their own house (Schweinhart et. al., 1993).

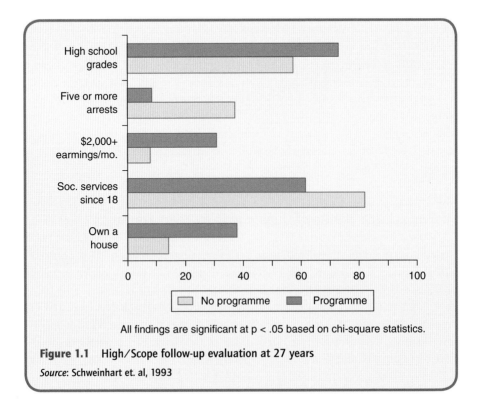

All findings are significant at p < .05 based on chi-square statistics.

Figure 1.1   High/Scope follow-up evaluation at 27 years

Source: Schweinhart et. al, 1993

Findings from the more recent EPPE project (Sylva et al., 2004) have further supported this position, finding clear links between the quality of early years educational provision and a range of intellectual and personal gains.

What emerges as significant about these particularly effective early educational environments is very much in line with the position that I have indicated so far. These environments offered real intellectual challenge in the ways we have discussed, requiring and allowing the young child to develop their self-regulatory skills. Within this kind of pedagogical approach, the child is put very much in control of their own learning. In the High/Scope regime, for example, the central model of learning is the 'plan, do and review' cycle. Each child plans their activities for the session or the day in a small group with an adult educator – often referred to as a 'key worker'. They then move off to carry out the planned activities, and later return to review progress again with their small group, again supported by their key worker.

This pattern of working also builds in purposeful adult–child and child–child conversations, which oblige and offer children the opportunity to reflect upon and talk about their learning. Sylva et al. (2004) particularly identified, within the highest-quality settings, the occurrence of episodes of 'sustained shared thinking' between adults and children, where adults supported children's ideas and helped the children to extend and develop them. As we shall see, providing opportunities for children to talk authentically about their learning is an important component in helping them to develop as self-regulating learners. This is also not just a matter of cognitive activity, but has important emotional and motivational elements. What all the high-quality early years regimes identified by Sylva and Wiltshire (1993) did was to help children develop what they term a 'mastery' orientation to learning and to themselves. Children in high-quality early years environments developed feelings of high self-esteem, with high aspirations and secure feelings of self-efficacy. Such children grew to believe that, through effort, they could solve problems, understand new ideas, develop skills, and so on. They felt in control of their environments and confident in their abilities.

Psychological Developments Required for Self-regulation

From my own work within the C.Ind.Le project emerged four underlying principles for a pedagogy of self-regulation, which arose from our analysis of effective practice, and which also relate strongly to current findings in developmental psychology. These principles are briefly explained and discussed here, and form the framework of the following chapters of this book, which deal in more detail with children's emotional, social and intellectual development.

1. Emotional warmth and security

Perhaps most fundamentally of all, in order to develop into effective learners within the school context, it is clear that young children need love and security. An important element in the tradition of early years education has always been a recognition of the need to consider the whole child. Children's learning and intellectual development is inseparable from their emotional and social development. In their early years, as well as mastering fundamental skills and understandings, young children are also forming their basic attitudes to themselves as people and as learners. The basic attitudes they form at this stage have major implications for their future educational progress and well-being as individuals.

An enormous body of research evidence collected by developmental psychologists supports this view. High self-esteem and feelings of self-efficacy are strongly related to educational success, and low self-esteem and what has been termed 'learned helplessness' are equally related to educational difficulty. It is difficult to attribute cause and effect here, but there is clearly a positive cycle of mutual interaction between self-belief and achievement and, sadly, a negative downward spiral associated with self-doubt and failure. Rogers and Kutnick (1990) have provided a useful survey of work in this area and its important implications for teachers.

Classrooms which support children's growing confidence as learners are first and foremost characterised by emotional warmth, by mutual respect and trust between adults and children, and by structures which provide emotional support (for example, clear and consistently applied rules). This kind of emotional atmosphere gives young children the confidence to play creatively, to take risks emotionally and intellectually, and to persevere when they encounter difficulties. In the absence of this kind of support, many young children will remain timid and passive in their general demeanour in the classroom, will be unwilling to try out new or unfamiliar activities and will give up on tasks as soon as they encounter difficulties.

A more detailed discussion of children's emotional development and the factors in the home and the school which impact upon it is provided in Chapter 2. This issue of emotional warmth and security also relates to aspects of social development and to children's experiences of play, which are reviewed in Chapters 3 and 4.

2. Feelings of control

Closely related to the need for emotional security is the need that all human beings have for feeling in control, both emotionally and intellectually. Feeling in control of their environment and their learning is fundamental to children developing confidence in their abilities, and to the ability to respond positively to setbacks and challenges. An early experiment carried out in California by Watson and Ramey (1972) illustrates very clearly this powerful aspect of human emotional development and motivation. It involved the parents of 8-month-old babies being given special cots which came complete with attractive and colourful 'mobiles'. The parents were asked to put their babies in the cots for specified periods each day for a few weeks. In some of the cots, the mobiles either did not move, or moved around on a timed schedule. But in other special cots the mobile was wired up to a pillow, so that the mobile would move whenever the baby exerted pressure on the pillow (see Figure 1.2). While the babies in the regular cots showed some interest in the mobiles, those in the special cots quickly learnt to

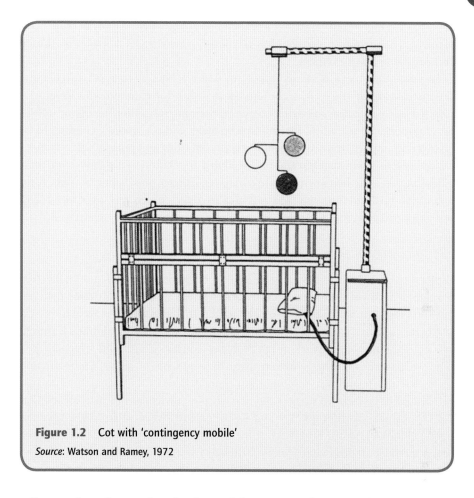

Figure 1.2   Cot with 'contingency mobile'

Source: Watson and Ramey, 1972

roll onto the pillow and make the mobile move, and expressed enormous glee every time the mobile moved (this is similar to the familiar game that babies love which involves them throwing something on the floor and an adult returning it to them; babies will repeat this for as long as the adult will play, laughing uproariously throughout!). At the end of the experiment, when the cots were taken away, most parents were perfectly content for this to happen. The parents of the babies who had experienced the special 'contingency mobiles' where the children had controlled the movement of the mobiles, however, offered to pay the research team large amounts of money to keep the cots because their babies had enjoyed these so much.

Feeling in control is a vital component leading to the development of what developmental psychologists term 'self-efficacy', which can best be described as a feeling of competence. Children with high self-efficacy are confident they can learn new skills, or understand new ideas, even though they might seem difficult at first. Indeed, they often positively enjoy a challenge and seek out difficult things to do. Children like this set their own challenges and learning agendas, and develop into highly self-regulated learners. Not surprisingly, a considerable body of research has demonstrated the clear relationship between feelings of self-efficacy and educational achievement.

As a consequence, it is vitally important that teachers of young children allow sufficient flexibility in their classroom organisation for children who have been inspired by a particular experience to pursue their interest. Allowing opportunities for child-initiated activities, for children to make choices, and for children to be involved in important decisions about classroom rules and procedures, enhances children's sense of ownership and responsibility in relation to the classroom, their fellow pupils and their own learning. As we shall see in Chapter 4, play is an important medium through which children develop feelings of control and self-efficacy (see Guha, 1987, for an excellent exposition of this relationship).

3. Cognitive challenge

While it is clear that there is an intimate link between emotional and intellectual development, love, emotional security and feelings of control on their own are not sufficient. Young children also need intellectual challenge. As we will review in Chapter 6, when we examine research about the processes of children's learning, as a consequence of the work of psychologists such as Piaget and Vygotsky, it is now widely accepted that children learn by a process of actively constructing their own understandings. An important characteristic of the human brain is that we all find enjoyment in mental activity; on the downside, this also means that we experience boredom quickly and easily, and this is most true when we are young children and our brains are at their most active. All the evidence suggests that a learning environment which challenges young children intellectually and stimulates them to be mentally active is one that they will enjoy, that will engage their attention and provoke learning. It also turns out to be crucial, once again, that the children are put in control. Such an environment will provide new experiences, embedded in meaningful contexts, opportunities for active styles of learning, involving children in problem solving, investigations and opportunities for self-expression, and, perhaps most crucially of all, opportunities for learning through play.

I well remember taking my own young children to look at one or two different schools when we were deciding where to apply for a primary school place. In the first one or two schools, the children hung back, hiding behind us while we spoke to their prospective teachers, and looking rather in awe of the large space that would be their classroom. In the last school, however, we entered the Reception classroom with difficulty as it was a complete Aladdin's cave, festooned and brimming over with children's paintings and models, and other exciting things to look at hanging from the ceiling, with all kinds of 2D and 3D displays adorning and bursting out of the walls, and with a cornucopia of fascinating objects to handle, games to play, toys to explore, and so on. As we spoke to the teacher, the children couldn't resist looking, then touching and finally playing with some of the exciting array of delights on offer and, at the end of the interview, it took quite a long time before we could persuade the children to leave this wonderful new world they had discovered. It was not difficult to decide which school was our first choice, where the children would thrive.

As we noted above, children will spontaneously set themselves challenges in their play and, given a choice, will often choose a task which is more challenging than the task which an adult might have thought was appropriate. Providing children with achievable challenges, and supporting them so they can meet them, is the most powerful way to encourage positive attitudes to learning, and the children's independent ability to take on challenging tasks. Research arising from Vygotsky's insights into children's learning (see, for example, Moll, 1990) has consistently shown that children learn most effectively when they are supported (or, in the metaphorical term coined by Bruner, 'scaffolded'), either by adults or by working collaboratively with their peers, in undertaking a task which would have been just too difficult for them to carry out on their own.

This issue of cognitive challenge arises in Chapter 4, concerned with children's play, and is also pursued further in Chapters 5 and 6, which review research concerned with the development of children's memories and understanding, and the different ways in which they learn.

4. Articulation of learning

Finally, it is clear that if children are going to become increasingly aware of and in control of their own mental processing, the processes of thinking and learning need to be made explicit by adults, and the children themselves need to learn to talk about and to express and represent their learning and thinking. Building in to regular practice within a classroom opportunities for the children to articulate their plans, and to reflect and comment afterwards upon their thinking and decision making during and after activities, is enormously advantageous in this regard.

There is good evidence to suggest that the processes of articulation and self-expression are important in helping children to understand and make sense of their experiences because of the processes of cognitive restructuring involved. The Vygotskian notion of learning through the co-construction of meanings in social situations and Bruner's notion of language as a 'tool of thought' are important here. In their explorations of young children's use of language in the home and school, Tizard and Hughes (1984) presented evidence of children engaging in processes of intellectual search through talk. The kinds of meaningful dialogues with adults that are likely to stimulate this kind of mental activity, however, they found to be much more common in the home environment than in the school. They argue that, as educators, we must find means of developing quality conversations between ourselves and the children in our classrooms. As mentioned above, this point has emerged again recently in Sylva et al.'s (2004) EPPE project findings concerning the distinctive prevalence of 'sustained shared conversations' in high-quality pre-school settings.

One of the clear disadvantages of the classroom environment relative to the home is, of course, to do with the adult–child ratio. For this reason, it is also important to stimulate challenging talk between the children. As a consequence, a range of educators have urged the more extensive use of collaborative group-work, peer tutoring and so on. Requiring children to work in groups to solve problems, carry out investigations or produce an imaginative response in the form of writing, drama, dance or whatever is potentially of enormous benefit.

In this regard, it is also important to recognise that the value of self-expression is not limited to the medium of language. Requiring children to transform their experiences into various 'symbolic' modes of expression is likely to aid the processes of learning. When children draw, paint, dance, construct, model, make music and, indeed, play, they are engaged in the active process of making sense of their world, of cognitive restructuring, in a way which is unique and individual to them, of which they are in control. The sheer vigour and enthusiasm with which young children engage in these kinds of activities is an important pointer to their significance.

Chapter 4 (in relation to some forms of play) and Chapter 6 deal in more depth with this vital relationship between language, self-expression and learning.

SUMMARY

Although I have attempted to separate out different elements in the psychological processes which relate to children's need for emotional security, feelings of control, intellectual challenge and self-expression, I must conclude by emphasising the powerful ways in which all these elements are of a piece. It is no accident that humans find activities which support learning immensely enjoyable. Adults at play, for example, are often enjoying the mental challenge of solving problems (crosswords, jigsaws, puzzles, games) or of expressing themselves (through music, art, drama). With enjoyment comes concentration, mental effort, motivation and achievement. Emotional security underpins children's confidence in expressing themselves and, in turn, self-expression builds upon and enhances children's sense of individuality and self-worth. A child who has experienced the excitement of finding things out for themselves or of solving problems is learning to take risks, to persevere and to become an independent, self-regulating learner.

Amongst the many challenges and complexities involved in teaching young children is the recognition that, as truly 'active' learners, they do not just learn what they are taught; rather, they learn what they experience. What I want to argue in this book, therefore, is that the effective early years teacher has to consider not only their own interpersonal style as a teacher, and not only the learning activities they devise and provide for the children, but also the entire classroom environment and ethos within which they and the children live and work.

It is always very sad to see the consequences of a poorly managed classroom: children standing around in queues waiting for a small amount of attention from the teacher; the children becoming over-dependent on adult support and unable to function without constant intervention; the teacher under constant pressure and frustrated that they never have time to do anything properly; equipment forever being lost in the general chaos; and so on. Lofty ideals about being child-centred, encouraging creativity and teaching the children to think for themselves all come to naught in such an environment.

In the last 20–30 years, we have discovered an enormous amount about children as learners which has direct and important implications for early years educators. What I have tried to do in this first chapter is to provide an overall rationale for the themes picked up in the book, based on research in evolutionary psychology – the evolution of the human brain – and in neuroscience, together with insights from recent and current psychological research with young children. This work supports ideas about the importance of emotion in learning, about human learning as a fundamentally social activity, and about the importance of real and meaningful experiences and contexts in learning. In the remainder of the book, I want to explore these themes in more depth and show how what we currently know about young children and their development can be enormously helpful in guiding us towards providing real excellence in provision, within which the strengths that all young children possess can be supported to help them develop as learners and young people.

References

DfEE/QCA (2000) *Curriculum Guidance for the Foundation Stage*. London: DfEE.

DfES (2006) *The Early Years Foundation Stage*. London: DfES Publications.

Featherstone, S. and Bayley, R. (2001) *Foundations of Independence*. Lutterworth: Featherstone Education.

Guha, M. (1987) 'Play in school', in G.M. Blenkin and A.V. Kelly (eds) *Early Childhood Education*, London: Paul Chapman.

Moll, L.C. (ed.) (1990) *Vygotsky and Education*, Cambridge: Cambridge University Press.

Rogers, C. and Kutnick, P. (eds) (1990) *The Social Psychology of the Primary School*, London: Routledge.

Schweinhart, L.J., Barnes, H.V. and Weikart, D.P. (1993) *Significant Benefits: The High/Scope Perry Preschool Study through Age 27*. Ypsilanti, MI: High/Scope Press.

Sylva, K. and Wiltshire, J. (1993) 'The impact of early learning on children's later development: a review prepared for the RSA inquiry "Start Right "', *European Early Childhood Education Research Journal*, 1, 17–40.

Sylva, K., Melhuish, E.C., Sammons, P., Siraj-Blatchford, I. and Taggart, B. (2004) *The Effective Provision of Pre-School Education (EPPE) Project: Technical Paper 12 – The Final Report: Effective Pre-School Education*. London: DfES/Institute of Education, University of London.

TDA (2006) *Qualifying to Teach*. London: TDA.

Tizard, B. and Hughes, M. (1984) *Young Children Learning*, London: Fontana.

Watson, J.S. and Ramey, C.T. (1972) 'Reactions to respondent-contingent stimulation in early infancy', *Merrill-Palmer Quarterly*, 18, 219–27.

Whitebread, D. (1995) 'Emergent mathematics *or* how to help young children become confident mathematicians', in J. Anghileri (ed.) *Children's Thinking in Primary Mathematics: Perspectives on Children's Learning*, London: Cassell.

Whitebread, D., Anderson, H., Coltman, P., Page, C., Pino Pasternak, D. and Mehta, S. (2005) 'Developing independent learning in the early years', *Education 3–13*, 33, 40–50.

Whitebread, D., Bingham, S., Grau, V., Pino Pasternak, D. and Sangster, C. (2007) 'Development of metacognition and self-regulated learning in young children: the role of collaborative and peer-assisted learning', *Journal of Cognitive Education and Psychology*, 6, 433–55.

Williams, J. (2003) *Promoting Independent Learning in the Primary Classroom.* Buckingham: Open University Press.

Chapter **2**

Emotional Development

Key Questions

- How are emotions related to cognitive processes?
- Why are positive early relationships important in emotional development?
- In what ways are early educational experiences an emotional challenge for young children?
- Why are some young children more emotionally resilient than others?
- How do young children learn to control their emotions?
- How can early years educators support children's emotional security and development?

Introduction: Emotions, Development and Learning

Within schools and other educational contexts, emotions are sometimes seen as a distraction, as an aspect of human behaviour which has to be coped with, but which is essentially irrelevant to the business of learning. In fact, everything we now know about the developing child powerfully suggests that this is a misguided and potentially highly damaging view. This is for at least two clear reasons. First, education at its best is concerned with the whole child, and learning to recognise and manage our emotions – what has sometimes been referred to as emotional 'intelligence' (Goleman, 1995) – is a fundamental life skill with enormous implications for a child's development. For example, the skills of friendship and the abilities required to work effectively in groups with others (to which we return in the next chapter) are crucially underpinned by the growing child's understandings and regulation of their emotions.

Second, learning, even if it is narrowly defined purely in terms of developing cognitive skills and understandings, is, by its very essence, a highly emotional process. Human beings, as we originally evolved over millions of years, were a successful species because of our ability to learn, think creatively and solve new problems. It is, therefore, no accident that we have evolved to enjoy learning and to be disappointed when we cannot understand something. Our emotional responses to learning powerfully drive our motivation to learn and to make the intellectual effort required to do so. If we seriously wish to help children develop their full potential as learners and as people, we must seriously attend to their emotional lives and development.

In her wonderful biography of Harry Harlow, Deborah Blum (2002) provides a chilling account of the consequences for young children of ignoring their emotional needs. She vividly describes childcare as it was advocated in the early decades of the 20th century (in large part by behaviourist psychologists), and of how it was practised in orphanages and in children's hospital wards in the USA (and in the UK and Europe) up to the 1940s and 1950s. The view then was that hygiene was the most important priority; shows of affection, and particularly those that involved any physical contact, were generally not helpful and to be discouraged. Children in hospital wards, for example, were often only permitted to see their parents for an hour a week and sometimes only through a glass screen. Gradually, the accumulating evidence of children failing to thrive under these conditions and, indeed, of becoming withdrawn and suffering from what would now be recognised as clinical depression, led to the recognition of the central importance of affection, and of loving relationships, for healthy development.

Two psychologists, Harry Harlow in the USA and John Bowlby in the UK, were particularly influential in establishing the crucial significance for development and learning of children's emotional experiences and relationships. Harlow spent his career researching the emotional lives of primates (mostly rhesus macaque monkeys) and his most famous experiment tested the proposition by behaviourist psychologists that children respond positively to their mothers because they are rewarded with milk. He set up various situations for baby monkeys where they had access to a surrogate 'cloth mother' construction which was warm and cuddly but provided no milk, and a 'metal mother' construction which included a milk bottle but provided no sensory comfort (see Figure 2.1). Disproving the behaviourists' hypothesis, when they had access to both mothers, the baby macaques typically spent the vast majority of their time cuddling up to the cloth mother and only visited the metal mother when necessary for a quick feed. Crucially, in addition, however, Harlow also placed some monkeys in the situation where

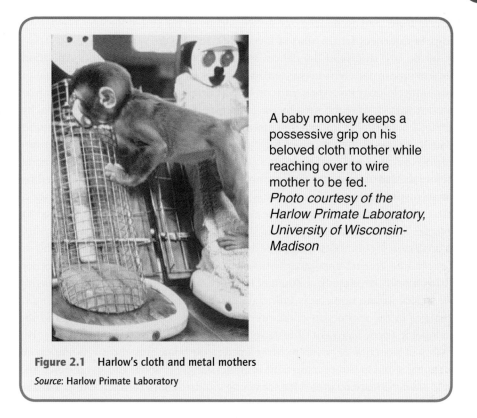

A baby monkey keeps a possessive grip on his beloved cloth mother while reaching over to wire mother to be fed.
Photo courtesy of the Harlow Primate Laboratory, University of Wisconsin-Madison

Figure 2.1 Harlow's cloth and metal mothers
Source: Harlow Primate Laboratory

they only had access to the metal mother, and observed how their behaviour differed. While the babies with the cloth mother appeared to be developing reasonably well, those with only the metal mother quickly became withdrawn and fearful. For example, when a new toy was placed in the cage, the cloth mother babies would come and explore it, showing the natural curiosity typical of young children which is so fundamental to learning. When a new toy was placed in the cage of a metal mother baby, however, they screamed with fear and cowered even further into the farthest corner.

The parallels with young children who are timid and fearful of new experiences, with the evident consequences for their learning, are very clear. In my very first class as a Reception teacher, I received one 5-year-old girl who showed all the signs of not having received much affection in her home situation (her father handing her to me on that first morning with the words 'give her a slap if she misbehaves'). She clung to me, constantly wanting physical contact, for several weeks at the start of the term, and would only engage in a very restricted range of activities (mostly playing in the water tray) throughout the whole of the first term. Although she gradually improved and became more confident and adventurous, and even made one or two friends by the end of the year, the damaging consequences for the start of her school career were very clear.

In the UK, studies of the deleterious effects of childhood institutionalisation, for example in children's homes and orphanages, and of even temporary separation of young children from their parents, as was common when they entered hospital for any reason, were reported by the child psychiatrist John Bowlby (1953) in his seminal book *Child Care and the Growth of Love*. For example, he reviewed studies which compared the outcomes for children who had experienced different care regimes in their early years. In one such study, children who had been fostered before the age of 9 months were compared with children who had been cared for in an institution until about 3 years 6 months and then fostered. By the age of 10–14 years, when they were assessed, the early fostered children showed an average level of social maturity and IQ. The late fostered group, by comparison, scored very low on both measures, being significantly more restless, unable to concentrate, tearful, unpopular with other children and craving of adult affection than typically developing children of their age, and having very low IQs averaging 72.4. This was an immensely influential book at a practical level, contributing to changes in the regimes in children's homes, orphanages and hospitals, and the increasing encouragement of fostering as an alternative to institutional care. His theory of 'maternal deprivation', developed in the book, was also a very important stepping stone in the development of understandings about the significance and role of affectionate relationships for young children, both for their emotional and their intellectual development, and has stimulated an enormous body of research concerned with 'attachment', to which we shall return below.

Modern neuroscientific research has also clearly demonstrated the strong links in the human brain between emotional and cognitive processes. The evolution of the brain can be divided into three rather general stages, which correspond to three rather general areas in the human brain (see Figure 2.2). The earliest emerging, usually referred to as the reptilian brain, consists of the brain stem and cerebellum and controls basic automatic (breathing, blood flow, etc.) and sensory/perceptual (smell, vision, etc.) processes. The second part to evolve, usually referred to as the mammalian brain, is the limbic system which is responsible for emotional responses, regulation and motivated behaviours. In the simplest, earliest evolving mammals this is an entirely unconscious set of adaptive processes concerned with 'fight or flight' responses. In later evolving mammals, including the primates, and in particular in humans, the limbic system has evolved to be intricately interconnected with the latest evolving part of the brain, namely the cerebral cortex. It is the cerebral cortex which is particularly highly developed in humans, and which makes consciousness possible, including our conscious awareness and regulation of our emotions.

The involvement of the frontal cortex in the management of social and emotional behaviour was first observed in studies of psychiatric patients who had undergone either full or partial frontal lobotomies in the 1940s and 1950s, where

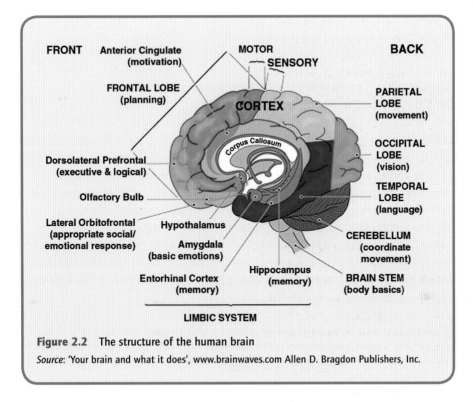

Figure 2.2   The structure of the human brain

Source: 'Your brain and what it does', www.brainwaves.com Allen D. Bragdon Publishers, Inc.

the connections between the frontal cortex were severed from the rest of the brain (a procedure now happily long discontinued!). Kolb and Taylor (2000), for example, record the case of a patient, Agnes, whose life was ruined by such a procedure. As well as losing the ability to plan or organise her life in any way, she also lost the ability to experience any feelings of emotion and was unable to produce or comprehend expressions of emotion through either facial expressions or tone of voice.

Essentially, what appears to happen in the normally functioning human brain is that information from the environment is fed from our sensory organs to the sensory cortex, which provides this information simultaneously to the amygdala and hippocampal formation (involved in the expression and regulation of emotions), and to areas of the prefrontal and cingulate cortex, which are known to be involved in higher-order thinking, decision making and so on. These areas, in turn, process this information and pass on instructions to the hypothalamus, which then produces the resulting motivated behaviours. A good example of the intimate interrelationships between emotional and cognitive processes contained within these brain processes concerns the anterior (or front) part of the cingulated cortex. This region of the cerebral cortex has been extensively researched and has been shown to be involved in both the recognition of cognitive conflicts (such as when two pieces of information suggest different actions) and the experience of pain or emotional distress.

Attachment: The Importance of Emotional Warmth, Sensitivity and Responsiveness

The early work of Harlow and of Bowlby stimulated an enormous amount of research concerned with the early emotional lives of young children. In this section, I want to briefly discuss two areas of this research, both of which have clear and significant implications for early years practice, and both of which relate to the importance of emotional warmth, sensitivity and responsiveness in supporting the emotionally healthy development of the young child. These areas of research relate to early emotional relationships, and to physical comfort and touch.

Bowlby's clear achievement was to establish the importance of what he referred to as early emotional 'attachment', which he famously defined in the following terms:

> what is believed to be essential for mental health is that an infant and young child should experience a warm, intimate, and continuous relationship with his mother (or permanent mother substitute – one person who steadily 'mothers' him), in which both find satisfaction and enjoyment. (Bowlby, 1953, p. 13)

Subsequent research has very much endorsed Bowlby's notion of the importance of attachment. However, this notion has been considerably developed and amended, particularly by the work of Mary Ainsworth and her colleagues (1978) and by Rudolph Schaffer (1977, 1996). Schaffer (1996) defines attachment as 'a long-enduring, emotionally meaningful tie to a particular individual' and lists the following characteristic features of attachments in young children. They are:

- *selective*, i.e. they are focused on specific individuals …
- involve *physical proximity seeking,* i.e. an effort is made to maintain closeness to the object of attachment …
- provide *comfort and security* …
- produce *separation distress* when the tie is severed and proximity cannot be obtained. (p. 127)

That young children do form these kinds of attachments is not in doubt. In his own early work, for example, Schaffer's observations of babies left in everyday separation situations (such as with an unfamiliar babysitter) revealed a marked change in behaviour around 7–8 months. Babies younger than that showed no particular preference for their mother; from around that age, however, the babies responded to their mother when she was physically present and showed separation distress when she was not. The well-known 'fear of strangers' behaviours also emerged around this time.

However, the research of Schaffer and others has shown that attachments are not formed solely with the mother, and nor are they necessarily the result of 'continuous' care. In a study of 60 infants through the first 18 months of their lives, for example, the majority had multiple attachments by that age, and some were more intensely attached to their fathers, even when they only saw them for part of the day. Indeed, cross-cultural studies have documented many societies in which multiple carers for babies and small children is the norm, with no apparent psychological damage. Bolwby's early claim that first attachments must be formed within the first two years of a baby's life has also not received support from subsequent research. While early attachment is clearly preferable, studies of institutionalised children who are subsequently fostered, for example, has shown that children are capable of forming later attachments, and that these are clearly beneficial. Even children subjected to severe deprivation, as in the case of the Romanian orphans discovered in the 1990s, some of whom were as old as 5½ years, were able, when subsequently fostered, to form emotional bonds with their new carers.

What has emerged as being highly significant for early attachments and for children's emotional well-being, however, is the quality and consistency of early relationships and interactions. This is more important than who they are with, how continuous the care is, how many carers there are or when the relationships are first formed. Not surprisingly, young children respond positively to adults who provide what Schaffer (1996) calls 'fun and playful stimulation' (p. 137) and to adults who are sensitively responsive to their needs and moods.

The assessment of the quality of attachment relationships, and their antecedents and consequences, was the major focus of the work of Mary Ainsworth, originally a student of Bowlby's. Together with a number of colleagues (Ainsworth et al., 1978), she devised and developed a technique known as the 'Strange Situation' which assesses the quality of the security of attachment between 12–18-month-old children and their mothers. This involves a procedure in which the children are separated from their mother, left with a stranger, left alone and then subsequently reunited with their mother (see Figure 2.3).

The pattern of behaviour of the child is observed during this process and, in a sequence of studies in the UK and in other countries, a typical pattern has been identified for the 'securely attached' child, and three further patterns have been identified for children who were deemed to be 'insecurely attached'. The secure child prefers their mother to the stranger, seeks physical proximity to their mother and is distressed when she leaves the room. However, this distress is quickly relieved upon the mother's return. Happily, this has been the most common pattern observed with a UK sample, as has also been the case with samples from a number of other countries, including Japan, Germany and the USA. Of the insecure patterns, the most commonly observed in the UK sample is referred to as 'avoidant'. Here the child shows no particular preference for the mother over the stranger and avoids contact with the mother on her return. In the 'resistant' or 'ambivalent' insecure pattern, the child is greatly distressed at

The procedure consists of a series of episodes involving collaboration between experimenter and mother. Throughout, the infant's behaviour is recorded either on video tape or by an unseen observer sitting behind a two-way mirror.

1 The infant and her mother are brought into a comfortably furnished laboratory playroom and the child has an opportunity to explore this new environment.

2 Another female adult, whom the child does not know, enters the room and sits talking in a friendly way, first to the mother and then to the child.

3 While the stranger is talking to the child the mother leaves the room, unobtrusively, at a prearranged signal.

4 The stranger tries to interact with the child.

5 Mother returns and the stranger leaves her together with the child.

6. Mother then goes out of the room leaving the child there alone.

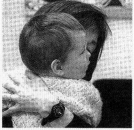

7 Stranger returns and remains in the room with the child.

8 Mother returns once more.

Each of these separate episodes lasts for three minutes at the most, but less if the child becomes very distressesd.

The video record is scored in terms of the child's behaviour directed towards the caregiver:

- seeking contact
- maintaining contact
- avoidance of contact
- resistance to contact

Figure 2.3   Ainsworth's 'Strange Situation'

Source: Cowie, 1995

the mother's departure, but then resists comforting by the mother on her return, partly seeking proximity and partly resisting or sometimes showing anger towards the mother. Finally, a 'disorganised' pattern has been identified in which the child appears confused and apprehensive, but shows no clear pattern of behaviour in response to the situation.

There has been considerable debate about the interpretation of these different patterns of behaviour and it is clear, for example, that the extent to which children are experienced at being separated from their mothers will have an impact on their response to the Strange Situation procedure. Perhaps for this reason, rather different frequencies of occurrence of the various insecure patterns have been found in samples in different countries between which the extent of separation from the mother normally experienced by a baby or young infant might vary (for example: a much larger proportion of Japanese children present a 'resistant' pattern than in the UK). Care also needs to be exercised in interpreting the results for children who have experienced a significant amount of day care, as apparently 'avoidant' behaviour could be interpreted as independence and self-reliance.

As regards the antecedents of patterns of attachment, there have been two main areas of research, which concern the sensitivity and responsiveness of the adult carer and the temperament of the child. Clearly, the quality of the interaction is dependent upon both of these factors. However, while it is well established that children do present individual differences in temperament from a very early age (for example, in activity level, distractibility, responsiveness) and consequently present different challenges to their parents and carers, the evidence generally supports the view that all children respond positively to sensitive and responsive interactions with adults, and are capable of forming secure attachments. Durkin (1995) has reviewed the extensive research in this area showing, for example, that children commonly form different attachment patterns with different adults, and that the caregiving style of the adult is a better predictor of the pattern of attachment than the child's temperament. An extensive collection of clinical studies, for example, has shown that parental stress and depression are commonly associated with insecure attachment patterns; however, the normal distribution of attachment patterns (i.e. with the large majority enjoying secure attachments) is found among children with behavioural problems. Further, where children have been removed from abusive or neglectful homes and fostered, highly sensitive foster parents have managed to achieve secure attachment patterns with these children.

As regards the consequences of attachment, it has been less straightforward to establish to what extent early attachment patterns are associated with long-term later outcomes. This is mostly a consequence of the fact that children who are securely attached in a responsive, caring family setting usually remain in that setting throughout their childhood, while children who are unfortunate to be in a neglectful, unresponsive or abusive situation as infants are also often still in them as adolescents. It is, therefore, very difficult to be sure as to whether the mental health and general well-being, the quality of social relationships, the success at school and so on enjoyed by an adolescent or young adult is a consequence of their pattern of attachment when they were infants, or of their current experience and emotional support.

There are, however, two particular lines of research which provide strong suggestive evidence of the potentially damaging consequences of insecure early attachment patterns. One of these relates to studies of the consequences of children experiencing long-term stress, which would normally be associated with insecure attachments. Gerhardt (2004) has reviewed extensive evidence of the physiological and psychological damage which can be caused by long-term exposure to high levels of the stress hormone, cortisol. This is produced naturally in the body, in the adrenil glands, when the limbic system that we looked at earlier detects some kind of crisis and wants to put all our systems on red alert – what is sometimes referred to as the 'fight or flight' response. This directs energy resources within the body towards dealing with the cause of the stress and away from regular physiological and brain functions, including, for example, the immune system and parts of the brain responsible for memory functions. This kind of response is precisely triggered by the kind of fear or uncertainty that can arise from the unpredictable social situations often associated with insecure patterns of attachment. As Gerhardt documents, it is a very necessary and useful mechanism to deal with short-term crises, but can have extremely damaging effects if an individual is in this state over long periods. Studies have reported a loss of responsiveness of the immune system, leaving stressed individuals more open to serious infection, a loss of behavioural control leading to increased levels of violence, and neurone loss in the hippocampus, affecting the ability to learn and remember. Most worryingly, this damage to the hippocampus also impairs control of the stress response itself, resulting in individuals who are increasingly prone to stress and anxiety when experiencing relatively minor difficulties or setbacks.

Gerhardt reports on one particular study, carried out by a team of researchers at the University of Wisconsin (Essex et al., 2002), which demonstrated very clearly this kind of effect of early exposure to stress. The team tracked 570 children from pregnancy to age 5. When they measured the stress levels of the children at 4½, they discovered that, of the children who were living with stressed mothers at that point, the children who were showing high stress levels were those whose mothers had been previously stressed or suffering depression when they were babies. In other words, these children now had a tendency to react at high levels to difficulties in life, whereas the children who had not previously experienced stressful relationships with their mothers were more able to control their stress response.

The other area of research relating to the consequences of early attachment patterns relates to an aspect of Bowlby's original theory of maternal deprivation, namely his notion that, through their early relationships, children develop what he called an 'internal working model' of social relationships, i.e. that children expect other adults to behave as their parents and early carers behave, and expect to have the same kind of relationships with them. There is some evidence to suggest that these models might even continue to influence the quality of an individual's relationships right into adulthood, and might even affect the kinds of relationships that mothers and fathers, in turn, go on to form with their own children. There is uncertainty about this evidence, because these studies often rely on adults' memories of their own childhoods, which can obviously be prone to error. However, what seems more certain, and is well documented and commonly experienced, is that children do generate expectations about adults and their relationships with them. This can be seen as a special case of their general preference for their environment to be consistent and predictable, to which we referred in the previous chapter when we were discussing emotional security and the need for feelings of control.

Importantly, what does emerge from this body of research is that, although there are clear cultural differences in child-rearing practices and although the antecedents and consequences of the quality of attachments are not always as clear-cut as Ainsworth might have originally suggested, nevertheless the establishment by young children of secure attachments to a range of adults is clearly beneficial. Many early years practitioners are, understandably, naturally drawn to form emotional relationships with the children in their care, but sometimes it is suggested that this is inappropriate, unprofessional or even dangerous. Given the research evidence which we have reviewed so far in this chapter, however, I would want to argue that this is a mistaken view. Handled with sensitivity, young children can only benefit from forming warm and secure emotional attachments to a range of adults who care for them, including those who work with them in early years settings. That the adults involved also derive pleasure from this is not an accident, but is part of our evolutionary heritage which has adapted adults to care for and be sensitive to the needs of young children. The children will undoubtedly benefit if we relax, relate to them naturally and enjoy it.

The other key message which emerges from the attachment research is that children's emotional well-being is not dependent upon the constant attentions of any one particular adult. Children naturally form multiple attachments at a very early age and appear to benefit from this. Early anxieties arising from Bowlby's work about mothers working and children being placed in childcare have been shown very clearly, by a range of research, to have been misplaced. What is important is the quality of the various relationships young children experience with adults (i.e. the warmth, sensitivity and responsiveness of the adults involved) and the consistency of those relationships. This last point, which derives from children's general need for consistency in their environment – witness their strong preference for routine and their love of hearing familiar stories endlessly repeated, just to select two obvious examples – has implications for behaviour by individual adults and between different adults. Young children expect there to be rules and for them to be consistently applied – we shall return to this issue in relation to parenting styles in the following chapter. They feel most secure when individual adults behave consistently, and when there is predictability and consistency between adults. It is for this reason that good communication between parents, other adult carers and adults working professionally in early years settings is vitally important.

I want to conclude this section dealing with emotional warmth and sensitivity by examining the research on young children and touch. This is an important area to discuss, as it relates to an area of current controversy in the early years educational world. I am reminded of Deborah Blum's harrowing account of the experiences of babies and infants in orphanages in the 1940s and 1950s where, to guard against infection, the staff were strictly forbidden to touch the children in their care. For very different reasons, early years workers are sometimes today advised to avoid unnecessary physical contact with children. I want to argue, however, that the evidence about young children and touch suggests rather strongly that this is an equally misguided view.

Early work in this area arose directly from Harlow's results with the cloth mothers. The baby monkeys clearly craved a soft touch (and young children's often compulsive love of their favourite piece of linen sheet, or most cuddly teddy bear, suggests that this does not just apply to baby monkeys!). Blum reviews a series of experiments with rats, for example, which showed that the production of growth hormones in baby rats, necessary for normal healthy growth, was stimulated by being licked by their mother and that, in fact, the effect could be successfully simulated by removing the mother and using a wet paintbrush! In relation to human babies, the breakthrough classic research was conducted in the 1980s at the University of Miami (Schanberg and Field, 1987), where a team of researchers systematically touched and massaged premature babies for 15 minutes, three times a day, and recorded 50% faster growth rates in the touched babies compared to standard isolated premature babies. The touched babies also showed cognitive and physical gains a year later. Figure 2.4 shows the rather moving case of premature twins, Kyrie and Brielle (reported by Diamond and Amso, 2008), which has led to the practice of 'double bedding' such children, with the same positive results. Subsequent research has confirmed that both active massaging and passive bodily contact, mainly by improving vagal (parasympathetic nervous system) activity and tone, are associated with a variety of emotional and cognitive benefits.

It is from this work that baby massage has become standard practice in hospitals, and has rightly become a popular focus for mother–baby classes worldwide. It has also stimulated a considerable body of research examining the beneficial consequences of touch between parents and children, between nurses and geriatric patients, between therapists and patients suffering from depression and a variety of psychiatric disorders, and between teachers and young children. In all cases, clear gains in relation to emotional well-being, self-esteem, motivation to persevere with tasks and so on have been recorded. In one such experiment, early years teachers were asked to either touch children on the arm, or not touch them, when they praised or encouraged them for any reason. Quite dramatic differences were recorded in the children's self-esteem and motivation and even in their learning. The message in terms of early years practice is clear. Young children will seek physical proximity to and comfort from adults to whom they are attached and will benefit very significantly both emotionally and cognitively from the stress-reducing consequences of this physical comfort and from active touching by these adults. Ironically, the evidence from a considerable body of research we have briefly reviewed in this chapter suggests that the impulse to protect children from possible harm by discouraging touch between young children and adults who care for them is likely to be extremely counter-productive.

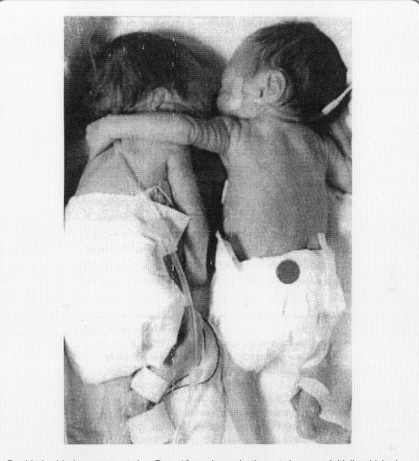

Double-bedded premature twins. Born 12 weeks early, these twins were initially whisked into separate incubators. Kyrie (on the right), the larger by over 2 pounds, slept peacefully, but Brielle (on the left) had breathing and heart-rate problems, didn't gain weight, and fussed when anyone tried to comfort her. Finally a nurse, acting counter to hospital regulations, put the two sisters together. As Brielle dozed, Kyrie put her arm around her smaller sibling. Brielle began to thrive. Sooner than expected, the girls went home. Today a handful of institutions use double bedding, which reduces the number of hospital days.

Figure 2.4   Double bedding with premature twins

Source: Diamond and Amso, 2008

Developing Resilience: The Development of Emotional Expression, Understanding, Empathy and Emotion Regulation

The first experiences children have of being cared for and educated professionally are, of course, very challenging emotionally and, not surprisingly, the transition from home to childcare setting or school can be a difficult time for many children. The issue of helping young children to manage these transitions, and of helping them to develop the personal resilience required to do so effectively, has been the subject of a good deal of research recently, and a number of excellent publications are available (Brooker, 2008; Cefai, 2008). Important messages which emerge from this work echo many of the ideas we have reviewed so far in this chapter. Children with existing secure emotional attachments have been shown to approach these kinds of transitions with more resilience, and adults and settings which put effort into managing transitions can help considerably in reducing the emotional stress experienced by children during this process. Because there are always cultural differences (of many kinds and degrees) between the world of home and childcare and school, young children's need for consistency and predictability in their world make extensive and sensitive communication between parents and the adults working in early years settings a vitally important ingredient in successful transitions. The factor which makes this all particularly important, however, and on which I want to focus in the last part of this chapter, is that it is during this same period that children are learning to express, understand and regulate their own emotions, and to understand and empathise with the emotions of others. Helping children to make another kind of transition, from being dependent upon adults to cope with and manage their emotions to being able to manage them themselves, to self-regulate, is a crucially important aspect of the work of early years carers and teachers. Fundamental to supporting this process effectively is understanding the nature of children's emotional development during this period.

Children are born, of course, experiencing emotions. The task ahead is for the child to learn to express them appropriately, to understand their own and others' emotions and to be able to regulate or control their emotions. This serves a number of purposes which are vital to the child developing into a socially skilled individual who can make friends, relate effectively to others – a topic to which we return in the next chapter – and deal with life's thrills and disappointments. Harris (1989) and Dowling (2000) have provided extensive reviews of the research concerned with young children's emotional development. What is clear is that there are strong biological aspects to our experience of emotions, but also, as is uniquely the case with so many aspects of human development, there are also strong cultural elements, i.e. aspects that are learnt within the social and cultural environment within which the child is nurtured. Thus, it is well established that, from early infancy, babies in all parts of the world express a range of basic emotions, including happiness, fear, sadness, surprise and anger; and the ways in which these basic emotions are expressed appear to be culturally universal – characteristic facial expressions arising from seven basic emotions (the five listed above, together with interest and disgust) have been shown to be produced and recognised even in remote tribes with no previous contact with the outside world. However, as we discussed earlier in the chapter, there are powerful links in the human mind between emotion and cognition, and very quickly, as the frontal lobes of the brain mature during the early years of life, these basic emotional experiences and expressions are influenced and increasingly controlled by cognitive processes of perception, understanding, re-appraisal and regulation. As the young child progresses through their pre-school and early school years, their emotions are increasingly responsive to how they interpret their experiences, what they perceive to be the intentions and feelings of others, and their understandings of the social conventions for displaying emotions in particular contexts. As with all learning, children learn to understand emotions through the situations in which they arise. Young children are also far less 'egocentric' than originally suggested by Piaget, for example, and surprisingly early in their development begin to understand the intentions of others, and to be able to sympathise with and show empathy towards others who are experiencing distress or unhappiness. These developments, connected with what has come to be referred to as the child's 'theory of mind', will be returned to in the next chapter.

What crucially emerges from all this research in relation to educational practice, however, is that, during their early years, children are very significantly engaged in beginning to understand their own and others' emotions, and can increasingly benefit enormously from opportunities to experience and discuss them. The development of understanding about emotions is a strong theme within children's imaginative role play – to which we return in Chapter 4 – but can also be supported very effectively through discussion of stories and real events within the home and in care and educational contexts. A range of evidence has supported the view that adults who discuss their own and children's emotional experiences with them help children to become more articulate and sophisticated in their emotional understandings and White (2008), among others, has usefully promoted the practice of 'circle time' activities in which these discussions are to some extent formalised and built in as routine elements within early years practice.

Such discussions, however, if they are to be effective, crucially depend upon the sensitivity and responsiveness of the adults who are involved in them. Routine discussions following some kind of pre-set programme (as is sometimes practised, with equal lack of success, under the rubric of Personal and Social Education in later years of schooling) are very unlikely to provide much of use to the young child. The responsiveness to young children's current experiences required crucially depends on the adults involved being sensitive to the children's experience and to their developing understandings. In this regard, an analysis by Gross (1998) of emotion regulation processes, all of which can be observed developing in the behaviour of young children during the early years, is particularly helpful. He lists five such processes which individuals use to manage and cope with their emotional experiences. I have set them out below together with examples from observations by my PhD student, Sue Bingham, to whom I am indebted for this important work:

1. Situation selection: people, places or objects can be approached or avoided

   Girl skips as she approaches the sandbox and then stops short and watches the noisy and boisterous play from the three boys already there; wary facial expression

as she watches for two minutes, occasionally turning around to see if the teacher is nearby; walks away frowning and finds alternative activity

2. Situation modification: similar to problem-focused coping

Boy fiddling with another boy's shoe as they sit on the rug during class circle time; the other boy pushes his hand away (facial expression of mild anger) but the first boy continues to touch the shoe; second boy puts up his hand and asks the teacher if he can move to another spot on the rug, which he does (facial expression now neutral)

3. Attentional deployment: involves distraction, concentration, rumination

Boy is waiting in the lunch queue with his tray ready; looks to the front of the queue and sees there is a hold-up; begins banging his tray against his leg (facial expression of mild anger), then places knife, fork and spoon on it and makes up a game, tipping the tray to make the cutlery slide from one side to the other without falling off (facial expression of mild happiness)

4. Cognitive change: involves modifying one's evaluations or appraisals of a situation

Girl is selected to choose a song for the class to sing; she chooses 'Ten Green Bottles' at which several children groan because they do not want to sing this; the girl blushes and puts her hands over her ears (facial expression of strong shame); whilst other children are singing the song she sits looking downwards, not joining in and squeezing her eyes together (holding back tears; facial expression of strong sadness); after two minutes she starts taking fleeting glances at the children sitting either side of her (facial expression of mild interest) and after a further minute she raises her chin and joins in the singing (facial expression neutral)

5. Response modification: affects the output of a re-appraisal process, and involves modifying one's behaviour in response to an emotional situation

Children all sitting on rug for 'registration'; girl (Helper of the Day) is asked by the teacher to select a friend to take the register to the school office; she looks round at her friends and several children put up their hand and make little sounds to indicate their desire to be chosen; the girl selects her best friend and a boy says loudly, 'Oh no, I knew it! That's not fair!'; the teacher looks around at him and raises her eyebrows in an exaggerated look of surprise/annoyance as she says his name in a 'warning' voice; boy changes his facial expression from a frown (facial expression of medium anger) to a smile (facial expression of forced mild happiness).

I'm sure anyone working with young children will recognise these kinds of situations and events, but it is also important to recognise their significance and the achievements they represent in relation to children's developing emotional expertise. As children move from the situation where they are dependent upon adults to cope with their emotions, to the situation of being able to cope independently, we do need to think carefully about how, as adults, we can best support this process. Research concerned with 'emotional education' suggests that it is always important to explicitly recognise and acknowledge children's emotions, rather than to deny or belittle them. This is particularly the case, of course, when a child is upset – telling them to pull themselves together is never helpful, since the child would clearly have already done this if they could. Whenever possible, taking time to discuss with the child how they feel, and why, and perhaps sharing with the child similar experiences of your own, or taking it as the starting point of a 'circle time' discussion a little later in the day, will always be a much more productive way forward. This kind of practice provides the child, over time, with the cognitive tools to learn to cope independently with these feelings.

As I have argued in the first chapter of this book, this needs always to be our guiding principle. If we are to help children to become effective learners and develop into individuals who have the personal and social capabilities to cope with life's challenges, we must always consider how to support them to take responsibility for their own learning and development. I want to conclude this chapter with an example of a particular piece of excellent practice from the C.Ind.Le project I mentioned in the first chapter. Figure 2.5 shows the start of a sequence in a nursery classroom where a 3-year-old boy was attempting to put on a fireman's jacket. His friend had already donned the policeman's jacket and helmet, and was waiting to play, so he was keen to put on the jacket as quickly as possible, but was having difficulty. This is clearly a situation in which he could easily have become frustrated, angry and upset. It would have been very easy for the nursery teacher we can see in the picture to have quickly put the jacket on him to avoid this potentially distressing situation. However, in fact, what she did was provide attention (talking to him about the problem and focusing her attention on him throughout), emotional support (smiling throughout, laughing positively and playfully when the jacket fell to the floor, encouraging him enthusiastically and expressing delight at each successful move) and clear visual guidance (demonstrating 'putting your arm in like this') which enabled the boy, after around two to three minutes of struggle and perseverance, to finally put the jacket on entirely by himself. The delight on the boy's face and his obvious sense of achievement made it clear that this simple little everyday event had been transformed by a piece of excellent practice into a very powerful piece of learning. It is no surprise to hear that every day, for the next two weeks, the first thing that this boy wanted to do when he arrived at the nursery was to put on the fireman's jacket. The lessons that this little boy had learnt from this incident in terms of perseverance, emotional control and self-efficacy are self-evident.

(a) the problem

(b) the happy outcome

Figure 2.5 Child putting on a fireman's jacket; supporting emotional development

SUMMARY

This chapter began with the fundamentally important role of emotions in learning, and the particular significance of this aspect of development for young children. We have seen how evidence from neuroscience and animal studies, together with studies of young children in situations of maternal and emotional deprivation, and observations of typically developing young children coping with their emotional experiences, have all helped us to come to understand the nature of emotional development and learning, and the role that adults can play in facilitating and supporting children to develop self-regulation in relation to their emotions.

Key themes to emerge from this work concern the importance of emotional warmth and responsiveness, of consistency in care, and of young children establishing secure attachments with significant adults. We have also reviewed the evidence suggesting that touch is an important part of these qualities in adult–child relationships. The processes by which young children come to recognise, express and regulate their emotions and their emotional expression have also been considered, together with the role that adults can play in this area. Finally, the chapter has looked at the issue of emotional responses to and involvement in their learning – children are faced with particular emotional challenges when they enter pre-school and primary school, which are often under-recognised. Providing emotional support to help young children make the transition into their new role as confident young learners is clearly of crucial significance, and we have considered the factors and elements of practice which are helpful in this regard. As broad guidelines for practice which we might derive in relation to this area, I would want to suggest the following:

- Young children will seek to form multiple emotional attachments to adults who care for them, and will benefit most in terms of their short-term emotional security, and potentially long-term developmental benefits, if the adults involved are open to forming these kinds of emotional attachments.
- Secure attachments will be most effectively formed with adults who are responsive, playful and sensitive to the children's emotional needs.
- As part of this process of attachment, young children will seek close physical proximity to the adults involved, and the adults can most productively respond to this, both in allowing passive physical contact and actively using touch when wishing to encourage, praise or express positive regard for the child.
- Children's emotional security is also supported by consistency in the behaviour and expectations of those who care for them, both within and between individual adult carers; clear expectations and routines and close and extensive communication between carers is, therefore, very beneficial in this regard.
- Adults caring for and educating young children need to be sensitive to the emotional challenges faced by young children, and also to their developing efforts to express, understand and regulate their own emotions and understand and respond to the emotions of others.

(Continued)

(Continued)

- It is important to explicitly recognise young children's emotions and, through example, discussion and emotional support, provide them with the cognitive tools to learn to cope with them independently.
- Events involving emotional difficulty for children should be regarded positively as opportunities for learning, rather than as an annoying distraction from the 'curriculum', and adults should attempt to support the children to learn from these experiences by resisting the temptation of resolving the difficulty for the children and, instead, helping them to experience the satisfaction of coping with the problem themselves.

QUESTIONS FOR DISCUSSION

- How can we tell if a child is or is not securely attached?
- How can we organise our setting or classroom to support children's emotional security?
- In what ways can we observe and support children's developing empathy and social understanding of others?
- When and how is it appropriate for adults to touch a child?
- How is it best to respond when a child shows emotional distress?

ACTIVITIES

A. Indicators of emotional security

One key indicator of a child's emotional security in any particular context is the quality of their involvement in their activities and their play. In this activity, therefore, the object is to make observations of children in your class/setting and assess their level of involvement. To do this, I would recommend using the Leuven Involvement Scale for Young Children (Laevers, 1994) which was adopted as part of the Effective Early Learning (EEL) programme developed by Pascal et al. (2001) and is briefly described here (it is also downloadable from the internet).

Each child should be observed for two minutes on three occasions in each of two sessions during one week, i.e. a total of six observations lasting a total of 12 minutes. On each occasion, you note whether or to what extent the child exhibits behaviours related to the following Child Involvement Signals:

- *Concentration*: the child is not easily distracted.
- *Energy*: the child invests a lot of effort in the activity.
- *Complexity and creativity*: the child is challenging him/herself, extending the task and developing new ways of doing things.
- *Facial expression and posture*: the child has a positive facial expression and posture displaying pleasure or intensity of purpose.
- *Persistence*: the child continues with the activity, even if it is difficult, for an extended period.

- *Precision*: the child shows special care in their activity.
- *Reaction time*: the child is alert and reacts quickly to events during the activity.
- *Language*: the child expresses enjoyment in the activity and the wish to repeat it.
- *Satisfaction*: the child displays a feeling of satisfaction with his/her achievements.

Based on these notes, you then rate the level of involvement shown by the child as follows:

- Level 1 – Low activity: the activity is repetitive or passive; there is a lack of cognitive demand; the child shows no energy; the child stares into space.
- Level 2 – Frequently interrupted activity: the child is engaged in the activity but half of the observed period includes the above characteristics of low activity or non-activity.
- Level 3 – Mainly continuous activity: the child is busy at the activity but at a routine level; there is low energy and concentration; the child is easily distracted.
- Level 4 – Continuous activity with intense moments: the child is at Level 3 but with moments of greater intensity, with more 'involvement' signals during which the child is not easily distracted.
- Level 5 – Sustained intense activity: the child engages in continuous intense activity; not all signals required but the child should show concentration, creativity, energy and persistence.

This provides a systematic set of evidence for identifying children who are more or less involved (and therefore emotionally secure) in your setting; it is also a useful tool for assessing progress in individual children, and for auditing your own practice, including, for example, the appropriateness of your provision. We know that if young children are interested in and engaged by the activities they are undertaking, and are consequently highly involved in them, in Laevers's sense of this term, then they will be able to learn from them.

B. Observation of emotional expression and regulation

Make notes over the first few weeks of the year, with a new class of children, of when you observe children expressing strong positive and negative emotions. Make a list of the emotions you see expressed and the contexts in which they occur. For example, you might note contexts such as: arrival, saying goodbye to their carer, going outside to play, changing for PE, playing in a group, sitting in assembly or other contexts leading to emotionally charged episodes.

Having identified a context, then observe a number of different children and attempt to identify how they cope with the strong emotion they are experiencing. Attempt to classify the strategies you observe under the headings described in the chapter: situation selection, situation modification, attentional deployment, cognitive change, response modification.

Use your observations as the basis for 'circle time' discussions with the class about when we feel strong emotions and how to deal with them. To keep things in balance, however, don't just focus on negative emotions. Discuss what makes us feel proud, happy or excited too! Share your own experiences and feelings with the children.

References

Ainsworth, M.D.S., Blehar, M.C., Waters, E. and Wahl, S. (1978) *Patterns of Attachment: A Psychological Study of the Strange Situation*. Hillsdale, NJ: Lawrence Erlbaum.

Blum, D. (2002*) Love at Goon Park: Harry Harlow and the Science of Affection*. New York: Berkley Books.

Bowlby, J. (1953) *Child Care and the Growth of Love*. London: Penguin.

Brooker, L. (2008) *Supporting Transitions in the Early Years*. Maidenhead: Open University Press.

Carter, R. (1998) *Mapping the Mind*. London: Weidenfeld & Nicolson.

Cefai, C. (2008) *Promoting Resilience in the Classroom: A Guide to Developing Pupils' Emotional and Cognitive Skill*. London: Jessica Kingsley.

Cowie, H. (1995) 'Child care and attachment', in P. Barnes (ed.) *Personal, Social and Emotional Development of Children*. Oxford: Blackwell.

Diamond, A. and Amso, D. (2008) 'Contributions of neuroscience to our understanding of cognitive development', *Current Directions in Psychological Science*, 17, 136–41.

Dowling, M. (2000) *Young Children's Personal, Social and Emotional Development*. London: Paul Chapman.

Durkin, K. (1995) 'Attachment to others', in *Developmental Social Psychology: From Infancy to Old Age*. Oxford: Blackwell.

Essex, M., Klein, M., Cho, E. and Kalin, N. (2002) 'Maternal stress beginning in infancy may sensitise children to later stress exposure: effects on cortisol and behaviour', *Biological Psychiatry*, 52, 776–84.

Gerhardt, S. (2004) *Why Love Matters: How Affection Shapes a Baby's Brain*. Hove: Routledge.

Goleman, D. (1995) *Emotional Intelligence: Why it Can Matter More Than IQ*. New York: Bantam Books.

Gross, J.J. (1998) 'The emerging field of emotion regulation: an integrative review', *Review of General Psychology*, 2, 271–99.

Harris, P. (1989) *Children and Emotions: The Development of Psychological Understanding*. Oxford: Blackwell.

Kolb, B. and Taylor, L. (2000) 'Facial expression, emotion, and hemispheric organisation', in L. Nadel and R.D. Lane (eds) *Emotion and Cognitive Neuroscience*. Oxford: Oxford University Press.

Kolb, B. and Wishaw, I.Q. (2001) *An Introduction to Brain and Behaviour*. New York: Worth.

Laevers, F. (1994) *The Leuven Involvement Scale for Young Children LIS-YC*, manual and videotape, Experiential Education Series No.1, Centre for Experiential Education. Leuven, Belgium: Leuven University Press.

Pascal, C., Bertram, A., Ramsden, F. and Saunders, M. (2001) *Effective Early Years Programme*, 3rd edn. University College Worcester: Centre for Research in Early Childhood.

Schaffer, H.R. (1977) *Mothering*. London: Fontana/Open Books.

Schaffer, H.R. (1996) *Social Development*. Oxford: Blackwell.

Schanberg, S.M. and Field, T.M. (1987) 'Sensory deprivation stress and supplemental stimulation in the rat pup and preterm human', *Child Development*, 58, 1431–47.

White, M. (2008) *Magic Circles: Self-Esteem for Everyone in Circle Time*. London: Lucky Duck Books/Sage.

Chapter 3

Social Development

> ## Key Questions
>
> - Are young children naturally sociable?
> - How do children's social understandings develop?
> - What are the consequences of children's differing social relationships with their parents and siblings?
> - Why are some children better at making friends than others?
> - How can early years practitioners most effectively support the development of children's interpersonal understandings and abilities?

The Social Nature of Human Beings

Human beings are intrinsically social animals. In one of Sir David Attenborough's many wonderful series for the BBC, *Life of Mammals*, the penultimate episode deals with primates: monkeys, apes and humans. This programme is very appropriately called 'The Social Climbers'. In it, Attenborough explains how, 10 million years ago, the climate of the planet changed and many forests died out and gave way to open grasslands. These new environmental conditions, he explains, supported the evolution of the great apes and, ultimately, homo sapiens. The particular characteristic which gave the great apes an adaptive advantage at this stage was their evolving ability to organise themselves in to large groups, i.e. their social skills. The programme goes on to show a troop of baboons, the complexities

Figure 3.1   David Attenborough demonstrating the relationship between brain size and size of social group

Source: Life of Mammals, episode 7: The Social Climbers, BBC, 2003

of their social life, and their emerging ability, in limited ways, to learn from one another. At the end of the programme, Attenborough lines up a row of plasticene balls which are ordered by size (see Figure 3.1). He explains that these represent the brains of different primates, and that there is a remarkably close relationship between brain size and the size of the typical social group in which they live: bush baby, brain tiny, group size 1; colobus monkey, slightly larger brain, group size 15; guenen monkey, again a slightly larger brain, group size 25; and, finally, the baboon, largest brain, group size 50. The social complexity of ever larger groups, and the survival advantages offered by such groups in open grassland environments, he argues, appears to have been a key environmental driver for the ever larger brains which evolved with each new primate species.

Human beings are certainly adapted to organise themselves in impressively large social groups, with complex hierarchies, rules of social behaviour and uniquely advanced capabilities for interpersonal communication and understanding. It is no accident, evolutionary psychologists argue, that we are attuned to be intensely interested in our fellow humans. Our love of human stories and dramas, of soap operas and, indeed, of gossip, are all evidence of this. Our essentially social nature is also at the root of the whole notion of education. As a species, we are uniquely capable of learning from one another to an extent which is qualitatively different from even the most advanced of the other primates. Experiments comparing observational learning in chimpanzees and human children, for example, have repeatedly shown the children to be infinitely superior in the speed with which they can solve a practical problem by observing successful performance. Observing a fellow chimpanzee successfully opening a box by moving a latch or turning a key, for example, hardly helps a chimpanzee at all – they learn to do something like this almost as quickly on their own. For the human child, however, the opportunity to observe the box being opened by another child or adult transforms the situation, often leading to an almost immediately successful performance. Hand in hand with this capability, while there are examples in other species where the young learn from their parents, we are the only species which deliberately sets out to teach its young.

The central importance of social competence in humans has two very clear consequences for young children's educational experience. First, developing social skills as a young child is particularly crucial for a happy and productive life as a school pupil, with all the social challenges of the pre-school and school classroom and playground. Beyond these immediate challenges, of course, developing the ability to understand others' points of view, emotions, motivations and cognitions is a vital life skill. In relation to this area, we will review research concerned with the young child's developing social relationships with parents, siblings and peers and the significance of these relations for their developing social abilities. This is a particularly crucial aspect of development, and one to which all who work with young children need to pay particular regard. For, not only is the development of social competence an important achievement in itself, but it is also fundamental to learning in many other areas, including emotional, motivational and cognitive aspects of development. Research concerned with the child's developing 'theory of mind' and friendship skills will be a particular focus here.

This leads directly on to the second important consequence of this aspect of our evolution, namely that we are adapted to learn most effectively in social contexts, and learning to learn with and from others is an important part of the agenda for the young child as a developing learner. We will explore the role of social context, relationships and collaborative learning later in Chapter 6, which focuses on learning and language.

In line with the continuing theme of supporting young children's self-regulation, the present chapter concludes by arguing that the adult's role can be most effectively concerned with helping children to become increasingly self-regulating in relation to their social development; work concerned with helping children to solve their own social disputes, for example, will be discussed. The chapter concludes with a discussion of implications for the early years classroom of what we now know about children's developing social competencies.

Children's Early Social Inclinations and Competencies

As in so many areas of development, some of the earliest work addressing fundamental issues relating to children's social abilities was carried out by the Swiss developmental psychologist, Jean Piaget. We will return to a fuller discussion of Piaget's vital contribution to our understandings about children's learning in Chapter 6. However, in relation to children's developing social abilities, it is informative to look at his work addressing perspective taking, or children's abilities to see situations from another person's point of view. This work includes the famous 'three mountains' experiment (Piaget and Inhelder, 1956) in which 4–12-year-old children were asked to look at a model of three mountains from one position and identify, from a selection of pictures, how they would look to a doll sitting in various other positions (see Figure 3.2). Typically, faced with this task, children under the age of 6 or 7 years old would select the picture which represented their own view of the mountains, rather than that of the doll. This was taken by Piaget as evidence of what he described as young children's 'egocentrism', or their inability to 'decentre', by which he meant their inability to see a situation from another's point of view.

However, subsequent research has shown that, in this instance, Piaget was wholly incorrect in his interpretation of these results. Young children's difficulties with his task seem to have arisen from their confusion about what they were required to do rather than from their inability to take the perspective of another. For example, in her seminal book entitled *Children's Minds*, to which again we will return in Chapter 6, Margaret Donaldson reports an experiment, devised by one of her PhD students, Martin Hughes, in which young children were required to 'hide' a naughty boy doll from a policeman doll (see Donaldson, 1978, Ch. 2 The Ability to Decentre). A diagram of the basic set-up of this task, showing the position of the child and of the policeman and some walls, in a

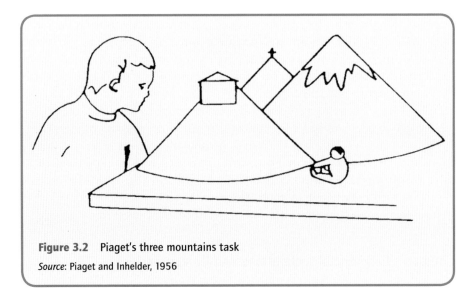

Figure 3.2 Piaget's three mountains task
Source: Piaget and Inhelder, 1956

simple cross configuration, is presented in Figure 3.3a. In different variations of this task, the child was either required to 'hide' a naughty boy doll so the police-man couldn't see him (i.e. in sectors A or C, but not B or D) or to say whether the boy could be seen by the policeman in a particular sector. In a further variation a second policeman was introduced (see Figure 3.3b), so that the only possible hiding place was sector C, where the boy was in full view of the child, but couldn't be seen by either of the policemen. Impressively, Donaldson reports that, for a group of children aged 3½ to 5 years, 90% of their responses to this problem were correct, clearly demonstrating their ability not only to see the situation from another point of view, but to simultaneously coordinate the views of the two policemen, both of which were different from their own. Donaldson attributes the children's success on this task to the fact that it makes 'human sense' to young children, who very well understand the idea of hiding, in a way that Piaget's three mountains task does not.

In fact, subsequent research has shown that children's abilities to understand their fellow humans, and to understand that they also have a mind like their own, and will have their own perspectives, as well as their own knowledge, beliefs, motivations and so on, are based on dispositions and abilities that begin to develop almost from the moment of birth. From a very early age, for example, young children show a fascination with other humans, and particularly human faces. As a consequence, a vast proportion of all research on early infant perception has concerned itself with early face perception. Indeed, some researchers have suggested that children are born with face-specific processing abilities. There is

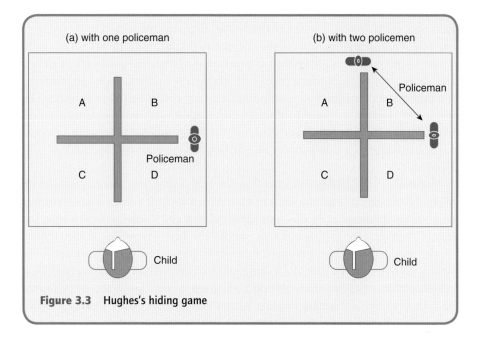

Figure 3.3 Hughes's hiding game

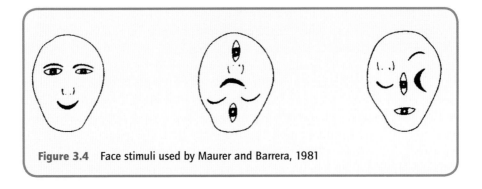

Figure 3.4   Face stimuli used by Maurer and Barrera, 1981

continuing debate within the research community, particularly in the attempt to distinguish infants' preference for complex visual stimuli from their preference for faces. Infants as young as 2 months, however, have been shown to discriminate between 'natural' faces and 'jumbled' faces. In the experiment by Maurer and Barrera (1981), for example, infants were shown drawings of a natural face, and two jumbled faces of equal complexity and with the same elements (see Figure 3.4). At 1 month old, infants looked at each of these faces equally, but by 2 months they looked for significantly longer at the natural face than either of the other two.

The dispositions and abilities of young children to interact with other humans have also been shown to begin to emerge very early in development. Two fascinating areas of research related to this aspect of development have examined young children's responses when adults do not interact with them, and when adults look or point at an object in the environment. Experiments related to these issues have shown that infants expect other people to interact with them by the age of 3 months (presumably based on their experiences of normal face-to-face interactions), and show clear signs of being disturbed when their mother, under instructions from the researchers, presents a 'still-face', remaining silent and expressionless. By 9 months, children are capable of following an adult's gaze and pointing gestures to establish joint attention on an object in the environment (in amusing contrast to the behaviour of a chimpanzee, who, in response to pointing, will look at your finger).

Andrew Meltzoff, an American researcher in this area, has carried out a series of studies related to learning by imitation which present some striking insights into young children's early understandings about, and dispositions towards, the minds of others. He has shown that, within the first few weeks of life, infants imitate mouth movements produced by another person but, very significantly, not similar movements produced by inanimate objects. Further, indicating clear evidence of an emerging understanding of others' minds, by 18 months children have been shown to imitate another person's intentions rather than what they actually do. For example, if an adult apparently attempts to place an object on a table, but accidentally drops it on the floor, or attempts to put something in a jar, but misses, children at this age are just as likely to imitate the 'intended' act as when they saw it carried out successfully. Children of this age have also been shown to be six times more likely to produce a target act after observing a human attempt, than an attempt carried out by a mechanical device (for a review of this work, see Meltzoff, 2002).

Theory of Mind and the Development of Psychological Understanding

These abilities shown by young children to understand that other human beings are different from other objects in the world because they have a mind, and therefore their own view of the world, their own knowledge, emotions and intentions, have been taken to be evidence of the early emergence of what has been termed a 'theory of mind'. The development of these understandings about others' minds has been the subject of an enormous research effort, particularly within the UK developmental psychology community, because it is recognised as crucially significant in the development of early social competence. This view has also been supported by extensive work suggesting that it is these mind-reading understandings and abilities which are impaired in children with autism (see, for example, Baron-Cohen, 1998 and Frith, 1989, 2008).

The classic test which has been very widely used to determine whether young children have achieved a basic 'theory of mind' concerns their ability to understand what have been termed 'false beliefs'. There are a number of types of false belief task, but they all put the child in the position where they know something, or have a piece of information, which is not known by another child, or by a character in a story or scenario. The child is then asked to predict what the other child or character will do in a situation where that piece of information is vital to making a particular decision. If the child can show that they understand that the other child or character will make the wrong decision, because they lack the vital information, i.e. hold a 'false belief' about the situation, then the child is deemed to have a basic 'theory of mind'. So, in the classic 'identity change' version of the task, originally developed by Gopnik and Astington (1988), a child is shown a Smarties tube and asked to say what they think is in it. Of course, the child says 'Smarties!'. When the tube is opened, however, much to everyone's amazement, it is discovered to contain pencils (see Figure 3.5). The pencils are then put back in the tube and the child is asked to say what their friend will think is in the tube when they are shown it. Most children up to the age of around 4–5 years of age will say 'pencils', and so are deemed not to have yet developed a fully constructed 'theory of mind' because they are not capable of predicting that their friend, who has not seen what is in the tube, holds a 'false belief' and will say 'Smarties', as they did just a few moments earlier.

Figure 3.5 The 'identity' change false belief task; the Smarties box unexpectedly contains pencils

Source: Gopnik and Astington, 1988

Another common version of this task, the 'location change' task, is more commonly known as the Sally-Anne task (see Figure 3.6). In this version, the child is shown a series of pictures in which Sally has a basket and Anne has a box. Sally also has a marble, which she puts into her basket before going out for a walk. While she is away, Anne moves the marble from Sally's basket into her box. When Sally returns, the children are asked to predict where she will look for her marble. In order to demonstrate a secure 'theory of mind', the child has to answer 'basket', showing that they understand that Sally will act on the basis of her 'false belief', although the child knows perfectly well that the marble is really in the box.

These simple experiments have proved to be very robust, consistently producing very clear results. However, as with many of Piaget's experiments, they have proved to be highly controversial, and the research this has generated demonstrates very well the difficulties and fascinations of researching with young children, or in any other way attempting to understand what they know, understand and are truly capable of at any point in time. Just as with many of Piaget's tasks, success at these false belief tasks has been shown to depend upon a range of skills and understandings which are quite separate from the central conceptual achievement which they are intended to assess. Success on these tasks has been shown to depend on verbal abilities (to understand the questions and articulate the answers), memory abilities and a level of inhibitory control (i.e. the ability to stop yourself saying the first thought that comes to mind, and to suppress that in favour of a second thought).

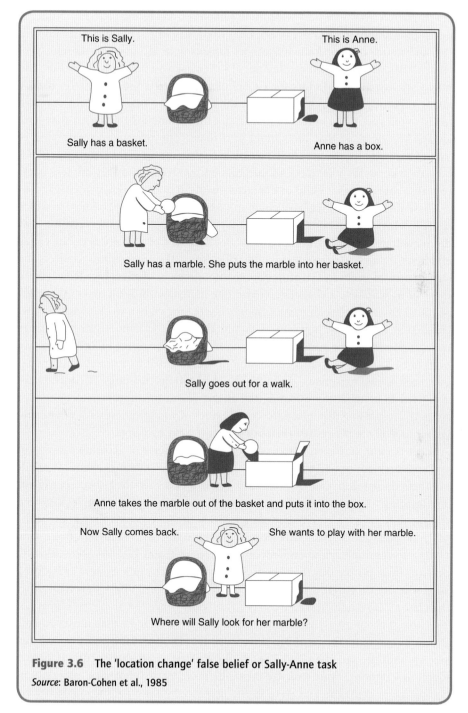

Figure 3.6   The 'location change' false belief or Sally-Anne task
Source: Baron-Cohen et al., 1985

In a recent study carried out with another of my PhD students, Demetra Demetriou, we found that the best single predictor of success on the false belief task was the children's 'source memory'. This is an aspect of what is termed 'metcognition', to which we will return in Chapters 5 and 6, and concerns children's developing ability to be aware of not only what they know, but how they know it (i.e. the source of their knowledge). So, for example, if I ask you the names of Henry VIII's wives and you can tell me, if I then ask you how you know this, you might say 'we did the Tudors for GCSE' or 'I watched a programme on the TV about it recently'. Young children under the age of 5 or 6 years, however, are most likely to tell you, when you have just taught them something new, that they have always known it, or that their mum told them. The relevance of this kind of 'source memory' for the false belief task is self-evident: if a child is not clear about how they know the vital piece of information involved, then they are less likely to realise that the other child or character involved does not know it either.

These various other aspects of children's developing cognitive abilities (to which we will return in subsequent chapters), of course, impact upon everything they do, including false belief tasks. This co-development of the vast array of young children's abilities, understandings and skills does make unravelling the effects and significance of each aspect of development extremely challenging. However, to those of us who love a challenge, it also one ingredient in what makes the study of young children's development infinitely fascinating. When working with young children as individuals, however, it should also make us cautious in jumping to conclusions about the causes of a young child's performance or behaviour. We need to be aware of the range of possibilities highlighted by research, and by our own professional experience, and to make observations in a range of contexts; we also need to be open to evaluating the effects of our attempts at remediation or support, recognising that, given the complexities of young children's development, we are unlikely to always (or even often!) get it right first time.

What is clear, however, is that, despite the difficulties of accurate assessment and measurement, young children's psychological understandings about the minds of others do develop, and this has clear consequences for their social behaviour and learning. A common finding in a number of studies, for example, has been that, as they grow older, children progressively describe people they know using psychological, rather than behavioural, descriptions. In a study by Barenboim (1981), for example, children between the ages of 6 and 11 years were asked to describe three people that they knew well, and their descriptions were categorised as to whether they were simply 'behavioural comparisons' ('Billy runs a lot faster than Jason'), 'psychological constructs' ('He's really conceited, thinks he's great') or 'psychological comparisons' ('Linda is real sensitive, a lot more than most people'). Figure 3.7 presents the resulting patterns of the data from this study. As we can see, up until the age of around 7 years, the children used almost entirely behavioural descriptions. From this age onwards, however, psychological descriptions became more common, and were in the majority by the time the children were around 9 years of age, However, it was not until the children were around 11 years of age that more sophisticated psychological comparisons began to emerge.

This research, however, probably under-estimates the level of understanding of young children about others' psychological states and characteristics. As often

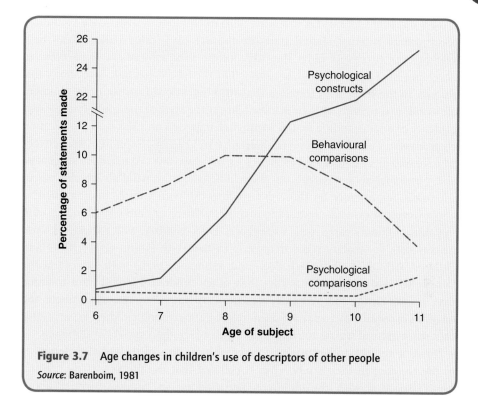

Figure 3.7   Age changes in children's use of descriptors of other people

Source: Barenboim, 1981

emerges in studies of young children's development, their ability or inclination to talk to a researcher about any particular topic generally can emerge some time later than their spontaneous talk on this topic or than behavioural evidence of their understanding in everyday contexts. Observational studies of children's spontaneous behaviour and talk concerning the internal psychological states of others, for example, have revealed that signs of empathy with others' feelings are present in children from a very early age. From as early as 10 months of age and up to around 18 months, this is mainly shown through imitative responses (such as crying when another child cries), but before they are 2 years old many children begin to offer support and help (such as by touching the person in distress, verbally expressing sympathy, offering comforting objects or fetching someone else to help). In a study of young children's spontaneous talk about others' internal mental states, Brown and Dunn (1991) showed that many children, by the age of 3 years, could comment on others' emotions, desires and motives, and were beginning to talk about how these internal mental states might be caused or changed.

The Impact of Early Social Relationships

What is striking about all these early developments in young children's social understandings, however, is that there are marked individual differences. So, while

Brown and Dunn found that around a third of children in their study could talk about others' internal mental states by the age of 3, other children can be a year or even two years older than that before they achieve the same point in development. Theory of mind, as assessed by the false belief task, also shows this pattern. In the study with Demetra Demetriou mentioned earlier, of 54 children, all within two months of their 4th birthday at the start of the study, five showed evidence of understanding on the 'identity change' task and seven on the 'location change' task. A year later, however, there were still 19 and 15 children, respectively, who showed no or limited understanding on these two tasks. While there are genetic and physiological antecedents of these differences, as with all developmental variations, importantly for those of us who work with young children, there is also a wealth of evidence indicating that these differences are related to variation in young children's early social experience. Thus, children with parents who use mental state vocabulary more frequently in their talk (Dunn et al., 1991) and children with older siblings (Jenkins and Astington, 1996) both succeed at the false belief task significantly earlier than other children. I would want to argue that, by examining this research, we can learn important messages about the qualities of social experience we need to be offering young children in early educational settings if we are to support and encourage their social development.

Dunn et al.(1991) investigated a range of indicators of the social experiences of the children in their study. They concluded that the differences they found were associated with the children's participation in family discourse about feelings and causality, with the verbal fluency of the mother and the child, with the quality of the mother's interactions with the child's sibling, and with the child's cooperative interaction with their sibling. In other words, perhaps not very surprisingly, the quality of the child's early social relationships, and the extent to which they are discussed and sensitively managed within the family, has a significant impact upon their early social understandings and, as we shall see, upon their own developing abilities to form and maintain relationships and friendships with others. This, of course, resonates very strongly with the work on attachment discussed in the previous chapter, and with the evidence concerning the importance of emotional warmth, sensitivity and responsiveness.

Quite independently of this work, there have been extensive studies of how parents and other care-givers vary in their styles of child rearing. This, of course, is a topic on which many people hold strong views and it is also one in which there are clear cultural differences. For a number of years, I ran an optional undergraduate course on parenting and I used to begin this course with two simple exercises. First, I would ask the students to rank in order a list of words describing qualities that they would want to encourage in their children when, and if, they had any. Words like 'creative' and 'independent thinking' would generally appear at the top of these lists. I would then show them the results from a study of the Nso people in Northwest Cameroon (Nsamenang and Lamb, 1995), where 'filial service' and 'obedience and respect' topped the list, and 'inquisitiveness' was rated as the least desirable characteristic. Second, I would hand out to each student a different book on parenting, each written by a self-proclaimed expert (as you will know, you can go into any bookshop and there are shelves full of these!) and ask them to review their book for the following session. What became immediately obvious, when the students reported back, was that diametrically opposed views were expressed in these different books, and with equally convincing enthusiasm and certainty. The point I wanted to raise through these initial exercises was that it is very difficult to assert that there is a 'right' way to bring up children. What is clear, however, is that parenting practices are generally adapted to support children in developing the qualities they will need to be successful members of the society in which they live – this kind of analysis is sometimes termed social Darwinism (interestingly, for example, there are strong links between parenting beliefs and styles and infant mortality rates).

However, within any cultural context, some parents are more successful in the task of providing beneficial early experiences for their children than others, and this is the nature of the individual differences we observe. Within so-called 'Western' modern technological and urbanised societies, the research on parenting styles has significantly revolved around the early work and theoretical model developed by Diana Baumrind (1967) in the USA. Based on interviews and observations with the mothers and fathers of 134 pre-school children, she developed a model of parenting styles which has been very largely validated by subsequent research, and which appears to predict significantly different outcomes for the children. She and other researchers examined a large number of dimensions along which parents might vary, including sensitivity, affection, directiveness, warmth, permissiveness, acceptance, punitiveness and responsiveness. However, two dimensions emerged which appear to account for the most significant aspects of parental behaviour, namely 'responsiveness' and 'demandingness'. Combining these two basic dimensions of parenting led to the description of four characteristic styles, as developed in an integrative review by Maccoby and Martin (1983) and reproduced in Figure 3.8.

Of the four styles identified, three are clearly dysfunctional in different ways, and have been shown to be associated with various kinds of behaviour in the developing children which are socially and educationally disadvantageous (Baumrind, 1989; Steinberg et al., 1994). 'Authoritarian' parents, who show little affection, are inconsistent in their demands and expect to be obeyed without question or explanation,

	Responsive	Unresponsive
Demanding	Authoritative	Authoritarian
Undemanding	Permissive	Uninvolved

Figure 3.8 Styles of parenting based on the dimensions of 'responsiveness' and 'demandingness'

Source: Maccoby and Martin, 1983

tend to have children who are low in self-esteem, surly and defiant, and who, on occasions, display high levels of interpersonal aggression. At the other end of the spectrum, 'permissive' parents are generally very responsive to their children, with lots of love and warmth, but are indulgent and set no clear or consistent standards or expectations. Their children tend to be impulsive and low in self-discipline, immature and easily influenced by others, and often find adjusting to school life difficult. The children of 'uninvolved' parents, who show little interest in their child's lives or welfare, sometimes to the point of neglect or abuse, are not surprisingly often the least well equipped to deal with the social and cognitive demands of schooling and life generally. Their self-esteem and levels of achievement are very low, and they are the most likely to be prone to depression and other emotional disorders.

By contrast, 'authoritative' parenting, which is high in parental responsiveness and in the demands and expectations made by the parents on the child, has been consistently shown, in a considerable body of research, to lead to positive outcomes for the child. The significance of responsiveness was, of course, independently identified by the attachment research reviewed in Chapter 2. Authoritative parents are the most emotionally warm and affectionate towards their children. In addition, however, they also set clear and consistent standards for their child's behaviour and convey high expectations of their performance. At the same time, they demonstrate clear respect for the child's developing need for autonomy and independence, and support the child's adherence to the standards and rules established through discussion and negotiation, explaining their reasoning rather than simply asserting their authority. This style has been shown to support children's developing self-esteem and self-regulation and, hence, their success as learners. In a series of studies in the USA, for example, Stephanie Carlson and colleagues (see Bernier et al., 2010) have demonstrated the role of early mother–child interactions in the child's developing self-regulatory abilities (measured using various measures of cognitive and emotional inhibitory control, to which we will return in Chapter 7). In particular, they have highlighted the role of maternal sensitivity (or responsiveness), of scaffolding (i.e. offering children age-appropriate problem-solving strategies) and mind-mindedness (the use of mental terms while talking to the child). Authoritative parenting has also been found to be associated with a range of positive outcomes in relation to children's social competence. As children, they most easily make relations with other children and adults, and are generally the most popular amongst their peers. In adolescence, the children of authoritative parents are more responsible and independent and significantly less likely than children experiencing the other styles of parenting to be involved in anti-social behaviour, or experiments with drugs, alcohol or premature sex (Steinberg et al., 1994).

Of course, with any categorisation of this kind, the four styles identified are massive over-simplifications, and almost certainly all parents act in each of these ways on some occasions (so don't worry if you have read this section with growing alarm about your own parenting – I'm sure it's not as bad as you think!). It is also the case that it is far more difficult to be an 'authoritative' parent when the adult concerned is experiencing personal stress, caused, for example, by the living conditions of poverty, by marital discord or by psychological illness. It is also certainly the case that an individual's parenting style varies in response to the temperament and behaviour of the child; we are all much more 'authoritarian' when faced with a child who is hyper-active, or when our children become teenagers and suddenly transform themselves from little angels into wayward monsters.

The serious point here is that I have not reviewed the research on parenting styles so that we can in any way 'blame' parents for any perceived deficiencies in their parenting capabilities. To start with, it has been shown in numerous research studies that adults tend to parent in the way they were themselves parented. Today's parents are also, I think it is widely accepted, often severely disadvantaged by the breakdown in the extended family, and the support and help that more experienced relatives can provide. The enormous market for books on parenting (to which I referred earlier), the size of the audience for television programmes on parenting, and the large uptake of parenting classes, are all testimony to the concern of the overwhelming proportion of parents to do their best for their children.

However, the research on parenting styles does, I believe, have some important messages for those of us who work with young children professionally. It gives us, to begin with, an extremely clear rationale for working with parents and, in any way we can, to support them in the enormously challenging task of child rearing. It also provides us with a clear basis on which to provide parents with evidence-based advice and, I believe, it also provides us with principles which can guide our own practice within the educational context.

Early Social Interactions and the Skills of Friendship

Adults are not, of course, the only other people with whom young children interact. There is a wealth of research concerned with their developing interactions and relationships with their siblings, peers and friends, and with the considerable impact that these early relationships have on their social and educational development. Young children show a particular interest in other children from a very early age and, contrary to the suggestions of some early research, have been shown to begin to establish friendships while they are still infants (i.e. within the first two years of life). In a study by Lewis et al. (1975) of 12–18-month-olds, for example, they investigated touching and looking behaviour when the infants were placed in a room with their mother and another infant–mother pair. Their results showed that, while infants of this age, predictably, stayed close to their own mother and touched her frequently, they looked mostly at the other infant (see Figure 3.9). Video observations of children in this age range in early years settings have also revealed them looking out for their friend to arrive, moving to play near to their friend, imitating one another's play, and so on.

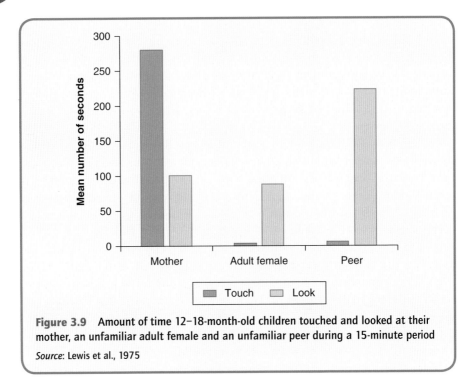

Figure 3.9 Amount of time 12–18-month-old children touched and looked at their mother, an unfamiliar adult female and an unfamiliar peer during a 15-minute period

Source: Lewis et al., 1975

Approximately four out of five children in the UK have siblings and, for these children, of course, it is within sibling relationships that they begin their earliest learning about social relations with peers. One of the most significant studies in this area has been that carried out by Judy Dunn and colleagues, who started making observations in the late 1970s of 40 families living around Cambridge. At the point of the first observations, each family had one child, usually just approaching their second birthday, and a second child was expected in a month or so. In the initial study (Dunn and Kendrick, 1982), observations and parental interviews up to the point where the younger sibling was 14 months were reported. The title of the book – *Siblings: Love, Envy and Understanding* – is indicative of the strong emotions that are often aroused within sibling relationships which can, of course, have lasting consequences. The follow-up study of these children when they reached early adolescence (Dunn et al., 1991), for example, found that children who had been unfortunate to grow up with a hostile or unfriendly sibling were more likely to be depressed, anxious or aggressive. However, it is clear that the vast majority of children derive enormous benefit from positive early sibling relationships, providing as they do a further early secure attachment opportunity and an initial arena for experiencing and developing understandings. As we noted earlier, children with older siblings appear to develop 'theory of mind' understandings earlier, for example (Jenkins and Astington, 1996).

As we also noted earlier, in the Dunn et al. (1991) follow-up study, it was noted that early 'theory of mind' achievement was associated with parents' use of mental state vocabulary. A further study of sibling relationships carried out in Japan has reinforced the significance of this aspect of parenting. Kojima (2000) reports an observational study of 40 sibling pairs in their home environments at the point where the two children were 2–3 and 5–6 years old. This includes an analysis of the mother's behaviour when the two children argued and were involved in some kind of dispute. A very striking association was found between the mother's tendency to diffuse the situation by explaining the actions or emotions of one sibling to the other, and the older sibling's positive behaviour to the younger sibling. There are clear implications here for professional practice, to which I will return below.

For all children, including those without siblings, however, there is clear evidence that the personal benefits and understandings which can be derived from sibling relationships, can also be derived from friendships with peers. Indeed, there is some evidence to suggest that the context of friendships may be even more significant. Various studies have shown, for example, that friendships can compensate for emotionally inadequate family relationships, and that children are more likely to take account of the other person's perspective, to compromise and to negotiate, when they are in conflict with friends than when they are in conflict with parents or siblings (see Dunn, 2004, for a review of the extensive research on children's friendships).

The significance and power of friendships in relation to young children's emotional and social development derives from the reciprocal relationship between these two facets of development. Friendships provide a powerful context within which children can develop social skills and understandings and, at the same time, the ability to form and maintain friendships depends upon these same abilities. Some children, of course, form friendships very easily, and the abilities which such children appear to possess will not come as a surprise, based on the research we have discussed so far on children's emotional development (in the previous chapter) and the recurrent theme of self-regulation which I am developing throughout this book. Thus, in a recent authoritative and wide-ranging review of research in this area (Sanson et al., 2004), the disposition to approach novel situations with confidence (arising, as we have seen, from secure emotional attachment) and the ability to regulate behaviour and emotions emerged as key characteristics of children with well-developed friendship skills.

These skills are beautifully illustrated in the extract below, taken from an early study by Corsaro (1979: 320–1) of young children's 'access strategies', i.e. the strategies they develop in order to join other children in their play and begin the process of making friends.

> Two girls, Jenny (4.0) and Betty (3.9), are playing around a sandbox in the outside courtyard of the school. I am sitting on the ground near the sandbox watching. The girls are putting sand in pots, cupcake pans, bottles, and teapots. Occasionally one of the girls would bring me a pan of sand (cake) to eat. Another girl, Debbie (4.1), approaches and stands near me, observing the other two girls. Neither J nor B acknowledges her presence. D does not speak to me nor to the other girls, and no one speaks to her. After watching for some time (5 minutes or so), she circles the sandbox three times and stops again and stands next to me.

After a few more minutes of watching, D moves to the sandbox and reaches for a teapot in the sand. J takes the pot away from D and mumbles 'No'. D backs away and again stands near me observing the activity of J and B. She then walks over next to B, who is filling the cupcake pan with sand. D watches B for just a few seconds, then says:

(1) D-B: We're friends, right? We're friends, right, B?
      B, not looking up at D and while continuing to place sand in the pan, says:
(2) B-D: Right.
      D now moves alongside B and takes a pot and spoon and begins putting sand in the pot.
(3) D-B: I'm making coffee.
(4) B-D: I'm making cupcakes.
(5) B-J: We're mothers, right, J?
(6) J-B: Right.

(This now triadic episode continued for 20 more minutes until the teachers announced 'clean up' time.)

In his analysis of this episode, Corsaro identifies a progressive range of strategies used by Debbie to join in the play and start the process of making friends. First, she places herself in the area of interaction ('non-verbal entry'). When this produces no response, she begins to circle the sandbox ('encircling'). Again, when there is no response, she enters the area and picks up a teapot ('similar behaviour'), but this is rebuffed. However, she persists and switches to a verbal strategy, saying 'We're friends, right?' to Betty ('reference to affiliation') and Betty finally responds positively to this move. Debbie then combines similar behaviour with verbal description, saying 'I'm making coffee' and from that point on the three girls play happily together. As we can see, this is a very impressive piece of strategic behaviour, requiring considerable social confidence and regulation of her behaviour by Debbie. These are not, of course, skills possessed by every 4-year-old. Children who were less socially confident might easily have given up after initially being ignored or rebuffed, and children with less well-developed self-regulation might easily have rushed in too aggressively, incited an argument and presented them-selves as someone to avoid.

Beyond the initial stages of friendship, a significant body of research has investigated the qualities and behaviours exhibited by children in maintaining their friendships. Children who maintain friendships are affectionate to their friends, are sensitive to their friends' emotions, and express enjoyment, caring and support appropriately. They notice and compliment their friends on their achieve-ments. They are also more cooperative, initiating joint play activities and respond-ing positively to other children's play initiatives, sharing equipment and toys, and agreeing more than disagreeing with their friends. They engage in a good deal of fantasy play with their friends (the role of which we return to in the next chapter). They develop intimacy with their friends, communicating their feelings and sharing personal information or 'secrets'. They are willing and able to delay getting what they themselves want (referred to as 'delay of gratification' in the research literature and, again, a form of inhibitory control). When conflicts arise, as they always do in any friendship, and as we noted earlier, they take account of the other person's perspective, are keen to compromise and to negotiate, and to resolve the disagreement amicably (see Dunn, 2004; Erwin, 1993; and Gallagher and Sylvester, 2009, for extensive reviews of these aspects of friendship skills).

As we can see, establishing and maintaining friendships is a highly skilled business and a considerable challenge for the young child, and for many young children, particularly when first entering the complex social world of the nursery or the school classroom, it is an area in which they will require considerable support. It is a particular challenge for teachers and carers working with young children to help them develop the abilities required in order to initiate and to maintain friendships. Given the significance of these abilities for the child as a developing individual and as a learner, however, it is difficult to think of a more important task for any professional working with young children.

SUMMARY

We began this chapter by noting the essentially social nature of human beings, and the consequent importance of children developing social competence. We have also noted that young children, not surprisingly, are very well attuned to the social world, taking a very early interest in other humans, and particularly other children. Very early in life, they begin to develop understandings about others' perspectives, intentions, emotions and knowledge states, quickly acquiring what is commonly referred to in the developmental psychology literature as a 'theory of mind'. We have also reviewed the qualities of early social relationships, between children and their parents, siblings and friends, which appear to support the development of social skills.

Key themes to emerge from the research and theory reviewed in this chapter have some clear overlaps with those related to children's emotional development. Once again, we have seen the significance of emotional warmth and responsiveness in parent–child relationships, and of consistency. To this we have added, particularly from the research related to parenting, the value of 'demandingness', of expecting and consistently supporting high levels of behaviour and performance from young children, thus enhancing their self-esteem. We have also seen the importance of what has been termed 'mind-mindedness', of parents and other carers engaging young children in discussions about inner mental states and feelings, particularly in handling situations where there is conflict between children. The research on friendships has again highlighted the importance of secure attachments, leading to social confidence, and of self-regulatory abilities in children if they are to develop the skills of friendship. We have reviewed the complex and demanding nature of friendship, and indicated some of the range of strategies and abilities that young children need to develop if they are to achieve a high level of social competence. I would want to argue that there are clear guidelines which emerge

(Continued)

(Continued)

from this area of research for practice within early years caring and educational contexts, as follows:

- Establishing an emotionally warm and supportive social environment in which children feel individually valued, and in which cooperation and mutual support are emphasised, will encourage the development of positive relationships.
- Setting high expectations of behaviour and performance, which are consistently upheld and reinforced, communicates to children that they are held in high esteem by significant adults, and supports their self-esteem.
- Discussion and negotiation concerning rules for behaviour towards other children and within the social group supports children's understanding of social rules, their feelings of autonomy and their development of self-regulation.
- Talk and discussion about inner mental states, including what individual children know, feel and think, particularly in relation to personally relevant concerns and events, helps children develop understandings about others' perspectives and motivations.
- Relations and good quality communication with parents of young children is of vital importance, providing their professional carers and educators with important information concerning their experiences in the home, and providing parents with support and guidance regarding child-rearing difficulties and concerns.
- Children can be significantly helped to develop the skills of friendship by those who care for and educate them modelling and discussing with them strategies to initiate and maintain friendship, and providing scaffolding and other support as they attempt to put these into practice.
- Disputes and conflicts between children should be taken as opportunities for their carers and teachers to present the situation as a problem to be solved by the children involved, to model processes of negotiation and compromise, and to otherwise support the children's developing abilities to resolve their own social disagreements.
- Opportunities should be provided for children to work cooperatively on joint tasks, to engage in cooperative and fantasy play, but also to withdraw into quiet places where they can escape the social whirl of the typical early years setting when they feel the need.

QUESTIONS FOR DISCUSSION

- Do we talk to the children in our setting about mental states?
- Why are some children more popular than others?
- Is it possible to teach the skills of friendship?
- How can we help shy children develop social confidence?
- What are the important elements of an 'authoritative' style of adult–child relationships, and to what extent does our practice embody this?
- Should we always intervene to help children sort out disputes that they find emotionally upsetting?

ACTIVITIES

A. Friendships

An interesting exercise to perform with a class of children is a process termed 'sociometry'. This is a simple way of learning about children's friendship relations; who the most popular children are, who have established and mutual friends or friendship groups, and which children are relatively isolated.

The process essentially consists of finding out, systematically, who children play with or who they would like to play with in the class. The former can be discovered by observing children for 10 seconds (in the order of the class register) repeatedly on a number of occasions, and in a number of contexts (in the imaginative play corner, on the carpet with the bricks, in the reading corner, in the outside area) over the course of a week. On each occasion, you simply record with which other child or children the child is playing. The second can be discovered by asking children to tell you (or another trusted adult such as their key worker, a nursery nurse or a teaching assistant) who they like to play with in the class; they are allowed up to three choices. These records of actual playmates or choices are then used to construct a 'sociogram', such as the ones below (from Clark et al., 1969).

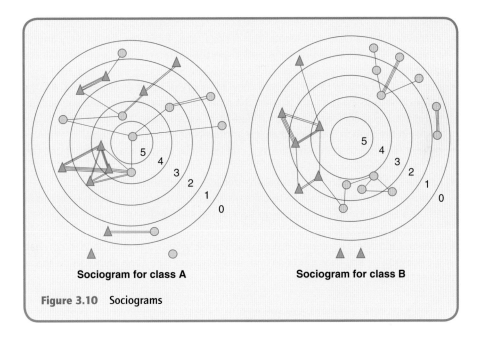

Sociogram for class A   Sociogram for class B

Figure 3.10   Sociograms

These sociograms are based on observations of children playing together in two different classes. The boys are represented by triangles and the girls by circles, and the lines joining them together represent the number of times they were seen playing together. The concentric circles show the number of play partners observed for each child, so the more popular children, or those with more play partners, are towards the middle, and the children with fewer or even no play partners are round the outside. In a sociogram constructed from choices, the general principle is the same, but each child's choices are recorded as lines, with an arrow on one end pointing to the chosen child. The children are arranged in the concentric circles according to how many other children have chosen them.

Such sociograms graphically represent patterns of social relationships within the class and tell you about the individual children and their friendship patterns; it clearly shows, for example, who has well-developed friendship skills, has lots of friends and is in the inner rings of the diagram, and who is towards the outside of the diagram and needs to be supported in their attempts to make friendships. It also tells you about the overall social 'ethos' of the class. Here, for example, the genders in class B are much more separated than in class A, where there is generally much more of an integrated pattern overall. Repeating this exercise at different points in the year can be a useful check on the social 'health' of the class of children. Clearly, reducing the number of social isolates and perhaps also those children who have only one clear friend in the group, on whom they are entirely dependent, are likely to be positive signs of improving social confidence and skills of friendship in the group.

B. Supporting children to resolve disputes

If two or more children are having an argument, try the following procedure to help resolve the situation and help the children learn something from it about how to manage their emotions and avoid distressing situations:

- acknowledge the children's emotions – for example, 'I can see you are very angry'; hopefully, if this is done in a calm and respectful manner, it will begin to calm the children
- ask each child in turn to explain why they are angry or upset or overexcited; ask the other child to listen carefully to what the other has to say; remain calm yourself, do not make any judgements and simply repeat or restate to each child in turn the key points in their report, showing that you acknowledge their point of view
- present the dispute to the children as a problem to be solved, again restating the two (or more) conflicting points of view
- ask the children to suggest possible solutions to the problem
- throughout, your aim should be to calm the situation. If a child becomes emotionally aroused again during the process, go back to the start and work through the process again (this is not often necessary)
- when a child offers a solution, restate it and put it to the other child or children; chair a discussion of any rival solutions until one is agreed, and then propose that this is what they do.

Usually, in most situations, this will lead to a happy resolution of the problem and, over time, the children will learn to use this strategy themselves when disputes arise.

References

Barenboim, C. (1981) 'The development of person perception in childhood and adolescence: from behavioural comparisons to psychological constructs to psychological comparisons', *Child Development*, 52, 129–44.

Baron-Cohen, S. (1998) *Teaching Children with Autism to Mind Read*. New York: Wiley.

Baron-Cohen, S., Leslie, A.M. and Frith, U. (1985) 'Does the autistic child have a "theory of mind"'? *Cognition,* 21, 37–46.

Baumrind, D. (1967) 'Child care practices anteceding three patterns of preschool behaviour', *Genetic Psychology Monographs,* 75, 43–88.

Baumrind, D. (1989) 'Rearing competent children', in W. Damon (ed.) *Child Development Today and Tomorrow*. San Francisco, CA: Jossey-Bass.

Bernier, A., Carlson, S.M. and Whipple, N. (2010) 'From external regulation to self-regulation: early parenting precursors of young children's executive functioning', *Child Development,* 81, 326–39.

Brown, J.R. and Dunn, J. (1991), '"You can cry mum": the social and developmental implications of talk about internal states', *British Journal of Developmental Psychology,* 9, 237–56.

Clark, A.H., Wyon, S.M. and Richards, M.P.M. (1969) 'Free-play in nursery school children', *Journal of Child Psychology and Psychiatry*, 10, 205–16.

Corsaro, W.A. (1979) '"We're friends, right?": Children's use of access rituals in a nursery School', *Language in Society*, 8, 315–36.

Donaldson, M. (1978) *Children's Minds*. London: Fontana.

Dunn, J. (2004) *Children's Friendships: The Beginnings of Intimacy*. Oxford: Blackwell.

Dunn, J., Brown, J., Slomkowski, C., Tesla, C. and Youngblade, L. (1991) 'Young children's understanding of other people's feelings and beliefs: individual differences and their antecedents', *Child Development,* 62, 1352–66.

Dunn, J. and Kendrick, C. (1982) *Siblings: Love, Envy and Understanding*. Oxford: Blackwell.

Erwin, P. (1993) *Friendship and Peer Relations in Children*. New York: Wiley.

Frith, U. (1989) *Autism: Explaining the Enigma*. Oxford: Blackwell.

Frith, U. (2008) *Autism: A Very Short Introduction*. Oxford: Oxford University Press.

Gallagher, K.C. and Sylvester, P.R. (2009) 'Supporting peer relationships in early education', in O.A. Barbarin and B.H. Wasik (eds) *Handbook of Child Development and Early Education*. London: Guilford Press.

Gopnik, A. and Astington, J.W. (1988) 'Children's understanding of representational change and its relation to the understanding of false belief and the appearance–reality distinction', *Child Development,* 59, 26–37. (Also reproduced in K. Lee (ed.) (2000) *Childhood Cognitive Development: The Essential Readings*. Oxford: Blackwell.)

Jenkins, J. and Astington, J. (1996) 'Cognitive factors and family structure associated with theory of mind development in young children', *Developmental Psychology,* 32, 70–8.

Kojima, Y. (2000) 'Maternal regulation of sibling interactions in the preschool years: observational study in Japanese families', *Child Development,* 71, 1640–7.

Lewis, M., Young, G., Brooks, J. and Michalson, L. (1975) 'The beginning of friendship', in M. Lewis and L. Rosenblum (eds) *Friendship and Peer Relations*. New York: Wiley.

Maccoby, E.E. and Martin, J.A. (1983) 'Socialisation in the context of the family: parent–child interaction', in E.M. Hetherington (ed.) *Handbook of Child Psychology, Vol. 4: Socialisation, Personality and Social Interaction*. New York: Wiley.

Maurer, D. and Barrera, M. (1981) 'Infants' perceptions of natural and distorted arrangements of a schematic face', *Child Development,* 52, 196–202.

Meltzoff, A. (2002) 'Imitation as a mechanism of social cognition: origins of empathy, theory of mind, and the representation of action', in U. Goswami (ed.) *Blackwell Handbook of Childhood Cognitive Development*. Oxford: Blackwell.

Nsamenang, A.B. and Lamb, M. (1995), 'The force of beliefs: how the parental values of the Nso of Northwest Cameroon shape children's progress toward adult models', *Journal of Applied Developmental Psychology*, 16, 613–27.

Piaget, J. and Inhelder, B. (1956) *The Child's Conception of Space.* London: Routledge & Kegan Paul.

Sanson, A., Hemphill, S.A. and Smart, D. (2004), 'Temperament and social development', in P.K. Smith and C.H. Hart (eds) *Blackwell Handbook of Childhood Social Development.* Oxford: Blackwell.

Steinberg, L., Lamborn, S., Darling, N., Mounts, N. and Dornbusch, S. (1994) 'Over-time changes in adjustment and competence among adolescents from authoritative, authoritarian, indulgent and neglectful families', *Child Development,* 65, 754–70.

Chapter 4

Play, Development and Learning

What is Play and Why Does it Matter?

Consider these scenarios:

- A young mother nibbles the toes of her 4-month-old baby while changing his nappy. The mother announces 'I'm going to get you ... I'm going to eat you all up' and the child laughs with delight, swinging his legs in the air. The mother laughs too.
- A 4-year-old walks alone down the garden path, stepping carefully on the largest stones and avoiding the smaller ones. He smiles as he goes.
- Two 5-year-olds are playing in a pre-school group. One is the 'nurse' and the other the ailing 'baby'. The nurse upbraids the other child, who is the younger of the two, scolding and bossing: 'Be quiet. Lie still. Here's your medicine.' The younger child begins to sob and hides his head under the pillow.

- Two 10-year-old girls are engrossed in chess. The dark-haired one ponders her next move for more than a minute, frowning all the time. The fairer partner stares intently at the board, fidgeting with her hair and biting her lower lip.

(adapted from Sylva and Czerniewska, 1985, p. 7)

We instantly recognise each of these events as involving play of various kinds, but it is very clear that whatever play is, it is a complex and many-faceted phenomenon. Psychologists have been attempting to define play and examine its role in children's development and learning for many years, but it has proved to be a remarkably elusive and complex phenomenon. Does it always involve saying one thing and meaning another, like the mother here who is not really intending to eat her baby? Does it always involve private meanings and imagination, like the boy here for whom the large stones are safe and the smaller ones dangerous? Does it always involve pretence, like the children pretending to be nurses and patients, and pretending to be bossy or upset? Does it always involve obvious enjoyment, or can play involve serious mental effort, as we see here from the two girls playing chess?

Establishing the psychological processes involved in play, and the precise nature of the development or learning which is supported by it, has proved to be enormously difficult. Play has turned out to be an extremely troublesome phenomenon to define and, perhaps because of its essential spontaneity and unpredictability, has presented significant challenges to researchers. Partly as a consequence of the relative lack of research in this area, until quite recently, opinions have varied between those who have asserted that learning in all aspects of development occurs most powerfully through play, and those (see Smith, 1990) who have argued that learning occurs through many kinds of activities, within which play may have a more limited role.

Today, it is almost universally accepted within the world of early years education that children develop and learn principally through play. However, while there is widespread commitment to the value of play for children's learning and development within the early years educational community, there is also evidence that practitioners often find it difficult to realise the educational potential of play in practice (see, for example, the study of Reception class teachers by Bennett et al., 1997). In large part, this appears to relate to an understandable lack of clarity about the essential attributes of play, the processes by which it supports development, and the aspects of children's learning and development which are crucially supported by it. In particular, there are long-standing confusions about 'structured' versus 'unstructured' play, and about the relative merits of child initiation and adult involvement (Manning and Sharp, 1977; Smith, 1990).

This confusion is not surprising, given the lack of clarity and precision in the developmental psychological literature related to children's play. However, there has been a considerable resurgence in research on children's play in recent years and I want to argue in this chapter that this more recent evidence gives us a much clearer view of the nature of play, of its purposes and the processes by which it influences development and learning. In turn, these more recent analyses provide very clear guidelines as to the nature of provision for play that is required to allow our young children to flourish in all aspects of development.

It is important to begin by establishing the significance of play for development and learning. The evidence now is actually quite overwhelming. To begin with, many commentators have remarked upon the ubiquitous presence of play in human behaviour, and particularly in the behaviour of human children. For any aspect of development that you can consider, there is a form of play. Janet Moyles, who has written prodigiously in this area, sets out this case very persuasively in the chart reproduced in Figure 4.1. Here she shows that for all aspects of development, including physical, intellectual, social and emotional, there are multiple forms of play. From an evolutionary perspective, when a form of behaviour is this prevalent across a whole range of activities in this way, the question naturally arises as to its purpose. Being playful clearly has had an adaptive advantage for humans, and has helped us to become a highly successful species.

Basic form		Detail	Examples
PHYSICAL PLAY	Gross motor	Construction	Building blocks
		Destruction	Clay/sand/wood
	Fine motor	Manipulation	Interlocking bricks
		Coordination	Musical instruments
	Psychomotor	Adventurous	Climbing apparatus
		Creative movement	Dance
		Sensory exploration	Junk modeling
		Object play	Finding out table
INTELLECTUAL PLAY	Linguistic	Communication/function/ explanation/acquisition	Hearing/telling stories
	Scientific	Exploration/investigation/ problem solving	Water play/cooking
	Symbolic/ mathematical	Representation/pretend/ mini-worlds	Doll's house/homes/ drama/number games
	Creative	Aesthetics/imagination fantasy/reality/ innovation	Painting/drawing/ modelling/designing
SOCIAL/ EMOTIONAL PLAY	Therapeutic	Aggression/regression/ relaxation/solitude/ parallel play	Wood/clay/music
	Linguistic	Communication/ interaction/cooperation	Puppets/telephone
	Repetitious	Mastery/control	Anything!
	Empathic	Sympathy/sensitivity	Pets/other children
	Self-concept	Roles/emulation/ morality/ethnicity	Home corner/service 'shop'/discussion
	Gaming	Competition/rules	Word/number games

Figure 4.1 Different types of play in school

Source: Moyles, 1989, pp. 12–13.

Jerome Bruner was one of the first psychologists to look at the evolutionary evidence. He pointed out, in his classic paper entitled 'Nature and uses of immaturity' (Bruner, 1972) that, as more and more complex animals evolved, with increasingly larger brains (see Figure 3.1, p. 38 in the previous chapter), the length of biological immaturity (i.e. the length of time the young were cared for by their parents) increased. This increase in the length of immaturity reflected the need for increased amounts of learning in complex animals with increasingly larger brains and, he noted, was paralleled by increasing playfulness. Furthermore, he argued, not only the amount but also the nature of the learning undertaken developed as larger brains evolved. Thus, as mammals evolved into primates, and as primates evolved into humans, there is an increase in problem-solving abilities, allowing greater 'tool use' and an increase in 'representational' abilities supporting the development of language and thought. Paralleling this, in mammals we see the emergence of physical play (mostly 'rough and tumble'), in primates we see 'play with objects' developing (chimpanzees will play with a lock and key quite happily for hours) and in humans we see the emergence of 'symbolic' forms of play which depend on our mental representational abilities and which include pretence, role play, artistic expression, playing games with rules, and so on. Based on this analysis, Bruner (1972) argued that humans have been a successful species because of our adaptability to new circumstances and our ability to solve new problems. Children's play, crucially, allows them to develop this 'flexibility of thought' because it allows them to try out different ways of looking at the world, different strategies to deal with problems and difficulties, and different ways of thinking, all within a safe context with no consequences.

Following on from these initial insights by Bruner, there has been extensive research on play in animals of all kinds, and a clear recognition that examining the evolution of play through species gives us extremely helpful insights into the psychological functions of play in humans, and particularly in children. Power (2000) and Pellegrini (2009) have both provided excellent reviews of this body of research, some of which we will return to in later sections of this chapter. Pellegrini, in particular, has concluded that, in animals and humans, play (as opposed to 'work') contexts free individuals to focus on 'means' rather than 'ends'. Unfettered from the instrumental constraints of the work context, where you have to get something done, in play the individual can try out new behaviours, exaggerate, modify, abbreviate or change the sequence of behaviours, endlessly repeat slight variations of behaviours, and so on. It is this characteristic of play, it is argued, that gives it a vital role in the development of problem-solving skills in primates, and the whole gamut of higher-order cognitive and social-emotional skills developed by humans.

Certainly, as I mentioned above, there has been a recent resurgence in interest in play amongst developmental psychologists, and considerable evidence has been provided for a close relationship between play and various aspects of development and learning. Bornstein (2006), for example, has reviewed the extensive evidence of the interrelationships between the complexity and sophistication of children's play, particularly their symbolic or pretend play, and their emotional well-being. The significance of symbolic play has been called into question by some commentators, mostly on the grounds of cultural variations. However, following an extensive review of the considerable current anthropological and psychological literature on culture and play, Bornstein (2006) concludes that 'pretend play (including role play and sociodramatic play) appears to be universal' but that it 'typically expresses concerns that are culture specific' (p. 115). So, for example, Gaskins (2000) found no evidence of 'fantasy' play amongst Mayan children in Mexico, as this kind of pretence would be considered to be untruthful, but did find extensive evidence of children enacting role-play scenarios of everyday Mayan adult life.

The relationships between play and cognition have been equally well established. Tamis-LeMonda and Bornstein (1989), for example, have demonstrated that infant habituation (an established measure of speed of processing which assesses how quickly an infant processes information about a new stimulus, and which has been shown to be significantly related to later cognitive development) predicts the amount of symbolic play individuals will engage in a few years later as young children.

Later in this chapter, where we look at each of the main types of play, we will examine the evidence of their specific impact upon development and learning. However, in this first section, it is important to review the impact on this whole area of research of the theoretical ideas developed by the Russian developmental psychologist Lev Vygotsky (1978). Vygotsky was born in 1896 (the same year as Piaget) in an area of Russia which is now Belarus, and sadly died young of tuberculosis in 1934, aged 37. His writings were suppressed in Stalin's era and not published in English until the 1960s. Since that time, however, his ideas about the processes of children's learning have been enormously influential. As part of this general trend, much of the recent work on children's play has been inspired by his insights concerning the mental processes by which play contributes to the effortful, intentional learning, problem solving and creativity required of children in educational contexts. We will return in more detail to Vygotsky's work, and the research it has inspired in relation to children's learning (and the role of adults in this) in Chapter 6. Here, however, we must consider two vital ideas that he developed concerning the role of play in development and learning.

First, Vygotsky specifically relates play to children's developing sense of control and self-regulation of their own learning. During play, he argued, children create their own 'zone of proximal development' (i.e. they set their own level of challenge), and so what they are doing is always developmentally appropriate (to a degree which tasks set by adults will never be). This also involves the notion that play is spontaneous and initiated by the children themselves; in other words, during play children are in control of their own learning. Guha (1987) has presented a range of evidence that this control element of 'self-regulation' is particularly significant in learning. For example, she cites experiments concerned with visual learning in which subjects are required to wear 'goggles' which make everything look upside down. They are then required to sit in a wheelchair and learn to move safely through an environment (i.e. a room full of furniture). The results of such experiments show that subjects moving themselves around the room (and having a lot of initial 'crashes') learn to do this much more quickly than those who are wheeled safely through the room by an adult helper.

Research by Russian psychologists who describe themselves as neo-Vygotskians has also explored the development of cognitive self-regulation and control relating to particular types of play. Karpov (2005) has provided a useful review of this work. For example, a study of 3–7-year-old children 'standing sentry' by Manuilenko (1948; reported in Karpov, 2005) supported Vygotsky's suggestion that children's use of verbal tools to regulate the behaviour of others was a significant factor in their development of self-regulation. Children standing sentry in a room containing playmates managed to stand motionless for significantly longer than when they were on their own. This appeared to be a consequence of the playmates 'monitoring' the 'sentry's' performance.

Second, Vygotsky argues that play makes a crucial contribution to the development of what he refers to as 'symbolic representation'. Human thought, culture and communication, he argues, are all founded on the unique human aptitude for using various forms of symbolic representation, whereby various kinds of symbols carry specific, culturally defined meanings. These forms of symbolic representation include drawing and other forms of visual art, visual imagination, language in all its various forms, mathematical symbol systems, musical notation, dance, drama, and so on. The links here with the subsequent evolutionary work discussed above are clear. Play is recognised in this analysis as the first medium through which children explore the use of symbol systems, most obviously through pretence. A particularly magical experience I was fortunate to have in relation to my own younger daughter, when she was around 1 year old, is relevant here. At this age, as is typically the case, Sarah was clearly beginning to use sounds (not yet quite words!) to carry meaning ('Mama', 'Dada', etc.). She was also, as it happened, playing a lot with a particular peg doll. I had watched her 'exploring' this doll as an object on a number of occasions. She looked at it while she wiggled it about, turned it upside down, dropped it and picked it up. She put it to her mouth, waved it about vigorously and banged it against other objects. Then, one morning, there was a new development. Sarah made the doll move as though walking along and made little humming noises as she did so. Suddenly, the peg doll was not just an object, she was a pretend little person, a symbol. This co-occurrence of the emergence of pretend play and the use of sounds to carry meaning (the beginnings of language) is widely reported, and clear support for Vygotsky's analysis of the involvement of pretence in the early development of symbolic representational abilities.

Vygotsky develops this argument further to suggest that pretence play becomes, therefore, a 'transition' from the 'purely situational constraints of early childhood' to the adult capability for abstract thought. So, as an adult, when you have had an interesting experience, upon which you wish to reflect, or a problem to solve, or a story to write, you have the representational abilities to do this in your mind, by thinking. Not having yet developed these abilities, however, the argument follows, children require the support of real situations and objects with which the ideas are worked out through play. So, when children have had a new or interesting experience, like a visit to the zoo, or to grandma's, rather than thinking about it, they act out significant events and ideas with their toys and with their peers. This kind of play, it is argued, both allows children to consolidate their understandings of their world and facilitates their development of the representational abilities they will use to think through ideas as an adult. The significant link here with research concerned with the development of children's thinking, problem-solving and creativity is the widespread finding of the significance of representational processes in these areas of development (to which we return in Chapter 6).

The 5 Types of Play

Given the general difficulty with defining play, and the recognition of its complexity, it is not surprising that there have been numerous attempts to categorise different types of play. As we have seen, Moyles (1989) suggests a categorisation based on the general aspects of development to which the play is related. Others have attempted typologies based on assumed purposes (exploration, imagination, skill development), on the area of learning involved (mathematical play, play with language, narrative play) on the equipment, materials or contexts used (sand play, computer play, outdoor play), on the individual or social nature of the play, and so on.

Within the psychological literature, the Swiss developmental psychologist Jean Piaget (often referred to as the 'father' of modern developmental psychology, and to whose major contribution we return in Chapter 6) was among the first to describe in detail distinctly different types of play, which he observed as they emerged at different stages during early childhood. So, he observed the early emergence of 'practice' play with objects in infants, then that of 'symbolic play', involving various kinds of pretence at around 1 year old, and finally, at around the age of 5 or 6, the emergence of 'games with rules'. Subsequently, various other types of play have been identified and different categorisations have been produced. However, in the contemporary literature the various kinds of play are generally divided into five broad types based upon the developmental purposes which each serves, partly arising from the evolutionary analyses to which we have referred above, and how each relates to and supports children's learning. These types are commonly referred to as physical play, play with objects, symbolic play, pretence/socio-dramatic play and games with rules. Although each type of play has a main developmental function or focus, arguably all of them support aspects of physical, intellectual and social-emotional growth and, in practice, any piece of children's playful activity will nearly always include elements of more than one of these types of play. A sound general recommendation, from all the available evidence, is that a good mix of experience of each of these types of play is likely to be beneficial to children's development. Within this section, I want to set out what the research evidence tells us about the typical developmental trajectories of each of these types of play, about their main psychological benefits, and about the implications for educational provision. For each type, it is also the case that children can play alone, with other children (of the same or different ages) and with practitioners, parents or other adults. (I will return to the important issue of the role of adults in the development of children's play in the final section of the chapter.)

Physical play

This type of play is the earliest to evolve and can be observed in most, if not all, mammals, and arguably some reptiles and amphibians. In human children, it includes active exercise play (jumping, climbing, dancing, skipping, bike riding and ball play), rough-and-tumble (with friends, siblings or parents/guardians) and fine-motor practice (sewing, colouring, cutting, junk modelling and manipulating action toys and construction toys).

Exercise play begins to emerge during the second year of life and typically occupies around 20% of children's behaviour by the age of 4–5 years. The evidence suggests that this type of play is related to children's developing whole body and hand–eye coordination, and is important in building strength and endurance. Useful general reviews of the research in this relatively neglected area have been provided by Pellegrini and Smith (1998) and by Smith (2010).

The most extensively researched aspect of physical play, however, is what is usually referred to as 'rough-and-tumble' play. This is prevalent among a wide variety of mammals and has been extensively studied in rats (see Pellis and Pellis, 2009), wallabies, cats, bears, elephant seals, cattle, monkeys and apes (see Power, 2000). In humans, it emerges slightly later than exercise play and is also typical among pre-school children although, like most forms of play, it continues in various forms right into adulthood. It includes chasing, grappling, kicking, wrestling and rolling on the ground and appears to have evolved as a mechanism through which children learn to control aggression. Although this kind of play causes concern to some parents and practitioners, it is easily distinguishable from actual aggression by the evident enjoyment of the participants, and appears to be wholly beneficial. The research evidence suggests that it is clearly associated with the development of emotional and social skills and understandings; for example, in human children, it is associated with the development of strong emotional bonds, or attachments, between children and their parents, and with school-aged children's abilities to understand emotional expressions (see Jarvis, 2010, for an excellent review of the research in this area and its educational implications).

Both exercise and rough-and-tumble play require very little equipment, but are clearly stimulated by opportunities to play outdoors. Young children, in particular, benefit enormously from being given the opportunity to play outdoors with other children and with adults, and should ideally be given this opportunity every day. Due to the differences in maturational rates, with girls generally maturing physically more quickly than boys in this age group, there are gender differences in these types of play, and boys may need these opportunities for a more extended period than girls.

I think it is very significant that when you ask adults to remember their experiences of play as a child, they nearly always particularly remember with great fondness their outdoor play. This may well be a consequence of the relative lack of adult supervision in outdoor play and there is a concern that today's children, largely through understandable concerns about safety, are over-supervised, arguably to the detriment of aspects of their development related to independence, resourcefulness and self-regulation. A general recognition of this concern among early years practitioners has led to a recent resurgence in interest in outdoor play, Forest schools, the outdoor schools in some areas of Scandinavia, and so on. A number of authors have written very helpfully and inspiringly about the opportunities afforded by the outdoor environment for child-initiated 'risky' play. I would particularly recommend Tovey (2007) and Frost (2010).

Fine-motor play refers to a wide range of activities which support young children's development of their fine-motor hand and finger coordination skills. These activities are often solitary, can be beneficially supported by an adult (such as sewing or construction) and, due to their absorbing nature, help children develop their concentration and perseverance skills. Children can best be supported in this area of playful activity by providing a range of opportunities, observing which activities they find most absorbing, and then providing further opportunities for this type of activity. Intriguingly, I have often observed that some of these kinds of activities are very popular with some of the most boisterous boys – I remember a number of examples of this from my own years as a practitioner. Boys who would routinely get into arguments and fights in other contexts, and who found it very difficult to settle at seat-based or pencil and paper tasks, would enthusiastically persevere all afternoon at sewing a pattern, or their name, or a simple line drawing coloured in (alien creatures or superheroes was a particular favourite!), with wool onto a piece of 'binka' (a textile material with a large weave providing clear spaces through which to pass the wool).

Play with objects

This second type of play, which is also widely observed in primates (see Power, 2000), in humans concerns children's developing explorations, as young scien-tists, of the world and the objects they find within it. It also has interesting and important links to physical, socio-dramatic and symbolic play. Play with objects begins as soon as infants can grasp and hold on to them; early investigative behaviours include mouthing/biting, rotating while looking, rubbing/stroking, hitting and dropping. This might be described as 'sensori-motor' play (see Smith, 2000) when the child is exploring how objects and materials feel and behave. From around 18–24 months toddlers begin to arrange objects, which gradually develops into sorting and classifying activities. By the age of 4 years, building, making and constructing behaviours emerge.

Play with objects appears to have a number of benefits related to the other types of play. As regards physical play, it is clear that manipulating, building and constructing with large and small objects are excellent ways of developing physical skills. Play with objects has also been shown to support the development of creativity (when it is associated with symbolic or pretence/socio-dramatic play). For example, while young children are making or building, they are also often developing a story or narrative.

Play with objects itself, however, seems to be distinctively related to the development of thinking, reasoning and problem-solving skills. It is in this kind of play particularly that young children appear to develop cognitive self-regulation abilities, as suggested by Vygotsky.

When playing with objects, children set themselves goals and challenges, monitor their progress towards them, and develop problem-solving strategies. Partly as a consequence of this theoretically strong link with important aspects of learning, problem solving with objects has been a reasonably well-researched aspect of children's play, and much of this research has been stimulated by a classic series of experiments carried out by Jerome Bruner and colleagues, in which he attempted to investigate his 'flexibility of thought' hypothesis (Sylva et al., 1976). The actual task used in these original experiments now looks very odd, as it involved children in fixing rods together with G-clamps and securing a hook on the end, in order to retrieve a stick of chalk from a transparent box without leaving their seat (see Figure 4.2). This makes more sense, however, when we recognise that it was based upon the popular 'lure retrieval' experiments of the time, which were being used to assess the problem-solving abilities of various animals, usually involving using some kind of tool (a stick) or combination of tools (a stick and a box to stand on) to retrieve some food. In the experiments with children, one group were given the opportunity to play with the objects involved (sticks, G-clamps, hook, etc.) while the other group were 'taught' how to use the objects in ways which would help solve the problem.

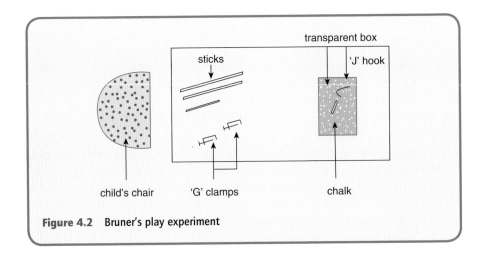

Figure 4.2   Bruner's play experiment

The results were very surprising. Consistently, after either the 'play' or 'taught' experience, when the children were individually asked to tackle the problem, the two groups performed at a similar level, in terms of numbers of children completing the task with total success. However, in the 'taught' group, there tended to be an 'all or nothing' pattern of responses, with the children either succeeding immediately by accurately recalling and following their instructions, or giving up immediately following an initial failure. By contrast, the children who had had the experience of playing with the materials were more inventive in devising strategies to solve the problem and persevered longer if their initial attempts did not work. The same proportion of children as in the 'taught' group solved the problem almost immediately, but many of those who didn't solved the problem at a second or third attempt, or came close to solving the problem, by trying out different possibilities. This result implies that, through playing with the objects, the children not only developed more flexible ways of thinking about the objects and how they could be used, but also developed more positive attitudes to problems and any initial setbacks.

As Smith (2006) reviews, these original studies were subject to some methodological criticism, due to the limitations of experimental conditions. The children also experienced either the play or taught condition for only a very brief period of time (sometimes as short as 10 minutes) and so it is difficult to be certain to what extent the results generalise to children's everyday life experiences. However, a number of studies have successfully replicated this original finding across a range of different kinds of task. I will describe below a study I have carried out myself with a colleague when we come to consider pretence/socio-dramatic play. Furthermore, subsequent work by Pellegrini and Gustafson (2005) concerned with object play, in which observational data was collected of 3–5-year-olds over an entire school year, demonstrated that the amount of playful exploration, construction and tool use in which children engaged, predicted their subsequent performance on a lure retrieval problem-solving task very similar to that used in Bruner's original experiment.

Play with objects is also particularly associated with the production of what is termed 'private speech', which consists of the production of a spoken self-commentary on the activity. This phenomenon, first identified by Piaget (1959), and very commonly observed in young children, was suggested by Vygotsky (1986) to have a self-regulatory function, helping the child to keep track of the goals of the activity, progress made and the relative success of different approaches. A number of research studies have demonstrated that the production of private speech during object and construction play is particularly related to the development of these important cognitive abilities. We will return to a discussion of this phenomenon in more detail in Chapter 6, when we look at the relationship between language and learning. Construction and problem-solving play, as indicated by findings from the Bruner experiment, are also associated with the development of perseverance and a positive attitude towards challenge.

To support this type of play, young children do not need a huge range of specialised toys, and already built toys can be less productive if they do not offer many opportunities for creativity and problem solving. The youngest children just need access to a range of basic everyday, natural and household objects and materials. One particularly successful strategy with children around 1 year old is to sit them down with a 'treasure basket' (see Figure 4.3 for an example) containing all kinds of interesting household and natural objects; containers (such as stacking cups), cardboard tubes, wooden spoons, sponges and strings of beads are particular favourites (see Goldschmeid and Jackson, 2003). This was first described by Elinor Goldschmeid, and is still sometimes referred to, as 'heuristic' play, i.e. play about how things work. Some other forms of object play are what might be described as 'messy play' and can perhaps be most easily provided outdoors (water, sand, digging in the garden); the kitchen or cooking area also provides rich opportunities for experimentation with objects and materials, with basic cooking activities a strong favourite. Play-Doh is an excellent basic modelling material (and can be 'home-made' in an exciting variety of shades and textures).

As young children develop, these basic exploratory and modelling activities can be supplemented with jigsaws and other puzzles and with all kinds of construction toys, including simple building blocks and well-made, flexible and open-ended manufactured building systems. Perhaps surprisingly, there is relatively little research on this later developing 'constructional' play – although Tina Bruce, among others, has collected some impressive evidence on 'block play' (see Figure 4.4 for some delightful examples from Huleatt et al., 2008). This is surprising as it is clearly a highly popular type of play with children at home.

Figure 4.3   Elinor Goldschmeid's 'treasure basket'

Figure 4.4   Blockplay

Arguably, however, the educational benefits of this form of play are significantly under-utilised within school contexts, perhaps because it comes to full fruition beyond the 'early years' when play provision within school is often very limited.

Symbolic play

We now come to types of play which are engaged in only by humans. The first two, symbolic and pretence/socio-dramatic, are very closely related, and there is much overlap between them. Indeed, many commentators use these terms inter-changeably. However, I think it is important to distinguish between playing with language, for example, which I want to refer to as 'symbolic' play, and using lan-guage to develop pretend scenarios or narratives, which I want to term pretence/ socio-dramatic. Although closely interrelated, I would argue that they are per-forming separate psychologically important functions.

As regards symbolic play, as I am defining it, it is no coincidence that, during the first five years of life – when children are beginning to master a range of 'symbolic' systems, including spoken language, various visual media, reading and writing, number, and so on – these aspects of their learning are an important element within their play. This type of play supports their developing technical abilities to express their ideas, feelings and experiences through language, painting, drawing, collage, numbers, music, and so on.

Play with language starts very early in life with children under the age of 1 year playing with sounds, and, as they grow older, particularly playing with the sounds of the language or languages they are hearing around them. This play is a very active process and quickly develops into making up new words, playing with rhymes, and eventually young children's love of puns and other jokes with language. This is an area which has been very extensively researched and there is a wealth of evidence that all these kinds of children's play with language are strongly associated with developing language abilities and, crucially, the ease with which young children develop early literacy. It has been established for many years, for example, that children's knowledge of nursery rhymes is a key predictor of early literacy. Christie and Roskos (2006) have provided a very useful review of the considerable research evidence linking language play of all kinds (both the purely symbolic and the pretence/socio-dramatic varieties) to the development of linguistic abilities, phonological awareness and early literacy. Having reviewed this extensive evidence, they argue very persuasively that approaches to literacy, in particular, which emphasise skills learning to the exclusion of playful approaches, are inevitably less effective, as they fail to capitalise on the boundless energy that children bring to their learning through the medium of play.

The role of children's drawing, painting and so on in their development has been less extensively researched. However, what research there is has made it clear that, certainly before they are fully literate, drawing and other mark making is a universal and important way in which children record their experiences and express their ideas. Vygotsky (1986) himself pointed out the very close links between early drawing and writing which is very commonly observed in young children's mark making. As with all play, in order to understand its meaning and purpose, with children's drawings it is important to observe the process rather than the product. Often, for example, young children's drawings are not a snapshot of one point in time, but record a narrative sequence of events, and the making of the drawing will be accompanied by a whole sequence of actions (without which the marks are completely uninterpretable) and dialogue performed by the child.

As a consequence, Thomas and Silk (1990) and Cox (1992) were among the first to warn that, in trying to understand children's drawings, it is important to observe the process, and not just the end product. It is also important to understand children's purposes in drawing. Research has shown that they are often recording what they know about objects, rather than attempting to represent how the objects look. In fact, the development of children's drawing skills in many ways parallels their linguistic skills. Through drawing, they gradually increase their 'graphic vocabularies' and their ability to organise graphic elements into a pictorial representation (a kind of 'graphic grammar'), and become increasingly able to use this mode of symbolic representation to express their meanings.

Figure 4.5 presents some examples of young children's drawings showing characteristic features which arise from these developments. The examples in section (a) illustrate the use of a piece of graphic vocabulary, namely 'how to draw a face', which is here applied to a man and his dog on the right side, and a man, his dog and his house on the left. You may know of the saying that we all grow to look like our pets, and here it is beautifully illustrated! The drawings in section (b) show issues that arise in children's attempts to structure and organise elements in their drawings – a kind of graphical 'grammar'. On the left are various solutions to the question of where to put the arms on a human figure (including just leaving them out, as they are too difficult). On the right are two examples of the solutions produced by children when asked to show specific information in their human figure drawings. In each case, the drawing on the left was produced in response to the request to draw a person. The top-right drawing was the modified version when asked to show all the teeth (with the head drawn wider to fit them all in) and the bottom-right was the result of being asked to show the buttons on the person's coat (with a much longer body drawn to accommodate these).

Section (c) illustrates various common features of children's drawings resulting from their intention to draw what they know, rather than to show what things look like. So here we have, on the left, various 'transparency' drawings where we can see the fly inside the spider, and the baby inside the mummy, and we can see all the lead around the dog's neck, through the horse to see the man's other leg, and through the table to see all the man standing behind it. On the top-right, the drawing of the horse and cart shows the use of multiple perspectives, so that each

Children's drawings illustrating:

(a) the growth of graphic vocabulary

(b) the growth of graphic 'grammar': issues with structure and organisation

(c) the intention to show what is known about an object rather than to show how it looks

Figure 4.5 Examples of children's drawings

Source: Cox, 1992; Thomas and Silk, 1990

object in the scene can be shown from its 'canonical' view, allowing the maximum information about it to be displayed. Thus, the horse and wheels are drawn from the side, but the cart is drawn from above and the people from the front (but orientated sideways to show their positions in the cart). On the right, this characteristic house and garden scene shows children's reluctance to overlap anything when drawing a complex scene, so each item has its own space and can be fully represented.

There is some evidence that children's visual literacy (i.e. their ability to understand pictures, photographs, diagrams, scale models, plans, maps, etc.) is importantly enhanced by their experiences of playing with a variety of visual media. Ring (2010) has for many years been researching the role of drawing as a tool for children to make meaning from their experiences and their worlds, and argues passionately and persuasively for the importance of continuous provision for playful drawing in early years educational settings. In our increasingly visual world, this would seem to be an eminently sound proposition.

Musical play is another very under-researched area, despite being a ubiquitous and highly significant form of play in all human cultures. From a very early age, children sing, dance and delight in exploring and making sounds of all kinds, with their own bodies and with all kinds of objects. An important series of insights into the fundamental significance of human 'musicality' has been provided by the work of Trevarthen (1999; see also Malloch and Trevarthen, 2009), who has extensively investigated early infant–mother interactions and demonstrated the role of the infant's innate response to rhythm and sounds in establishing early communicative abilities. A part of this response also appears to relate to children's more general interest in patterns of all kinds, which seems to underlay both mathematical and aesthetic developments. Pound (2010) has provided a recent review of research concerned with early musical development, and argued persuasively that musical play supports children's developing abilities in relation to social interaction, communication, emotion understanding, memory, self-regulation and creativity.

Self-evidently, since a primary purpose of our human capacity for symbolic representation is to facilitate improved communication, adults and other children have an important role in encouraging and supporting this area of children's play and development. Playing with sounds and music, making up rhymes, enjoying young children's playfulness with language and joining in, drawing and painting with young children, all encourage and support the quality of children's play and learning in these areas. The one final and important point to make is that, as a consequence of societal and educational pressures, this is often an aspect of development, particularly relating to literacy, about which parents and practitioners are anxious. The research strongly suggests, however, that a playful and supportive style of parenting and teaching is far more productive in terms of children's language and literacy development than an anxious and correcting style. We will return to this important issue of the adult's role in children's play in the final section of this chapter.

Pretence/socio-dramatic play

From the age of around 1 year, and certainly all through the early years and primary age range, the various manifestations of pretence and socio-dramatic play are perhaps the most common type of play of all. I certainly remember that my own daughters, right up until they became teenagers, appeared to be constantly in a world of imagination and make-believe. I have many happy memories of arriving home from work to be greeted by my eldest daughter, Elisabeth, festooned in various of my wife's cast-offs, old tea towels, glitter, ribbons, etc. 'Hello, Lizzie,' I would volunteer, only to be severely reprimanded with something along the lines of 'I'm not Lizzie, I'm Princess Smartypants, and you should kneel in my presence, or I'll cut off your head!' As well as dressing up and role playing (fantasy and real-world), this type of play includes all forms of pretence – playing with dolls, puppets and action figures, playing with mini-worlds, playing with an imaginary friend and, arguably, playing with pets (when human emotions and motivations are consistently attributed to even the simplest of creatures). It typically emerges in children during their second year as solitary pretence play, where they use objects to pretend they are something else, then evolves into dressing up and pretending the child is someone or something else (for example, a mummy, Superman, a dog). By 4–5 years of age, this play has become cooperative and social and involves role play and developing stories or narratives.

This is the most researched form of play, partly because of its well-established significance for the development of children's imagination and thinking skills. High-quality pretend play has repeatedly been shown to be very closely associated with cognitive, social and academic development. Studies have reported the impact of playworld experience on narrative skills in 5–7-year-olds, of pretence play on deductive reasoning and 'theory of mind' (the basis of social understanding, as discussed in Chapter 3) and of socio-dramatic play on improved 'self-regulation' among young children who are prone to be highly impulsive. This type of play is also strongly associated with social and emotional learning, including developing an understanding of others; playing with and caring for pets is also included in this type of play because of its well-established benefits in relation to emotional development.

Empirical support for Vygotsky's argument regarding the link between pretend play and the development of symbolic representational abilities in children has come from a range of studies. Dyachenko (1980; reported in Karpov, 2005) showed that 5–6-year-olds' ability to retell a story was significantly enhanced by the use of representational objects such as sticks, paper cut-outs, etc., and that their ability to retell a story without the use of these objects was subsequently enhanced. Berk et al. (2006) reported a series of observational studies of 2–6-year-old children in which they recorded the incidence of 'private speech'. As we discussed earlier, in Vygotskian theory young children's tendency to talk to themselves, or self-commentate, while they are undertaking a task, is of great significance, as he argues that such speech is an important step in the processes by which children learn to represent ideas to themselves in language and learn to use language to self-regulate their activities. Berk and her colleagues found particularly high levels of private speech and verbal self-regulation among 2–6-year-old children during open-ended, make-believe or pretend play.

In a study that I carried out myself with a teacher colleague (Whitebread and Jameson, 2010), partly inspired by the Dyachenko study reported above, a group of able 6–7-year-olds were asked to produce oral and written stories after they had been read a story and had experience of Storysacks consisting of story dolls and props (see Figure 4.6 for some examples) under 'play' and 'taught' conditions,

Figure 4.6   'If Only' and 'Enormous Crocodile' Storysacks

following the model of the original Sylva et al. (1976) study. It is important to note, however, that in order to address some of the methodological criticisms of the original study, we also included a 'control' condition, where the children neither played with nor were taught using the Storysack materials. Also, unlike the original study, we used a 'repeated measures' design in which the same 35 children experienced each of the three different pedagogical conditions.

The essence of a good story, of course, is that it involves a series of problems or conflicts, which are then happily resolved. Analysis of the children's written stories arising from the three conditions showed that in the 'play' condition, the children included about the same number of conflicts as in the 'taught' condition, and more than in the 'control' condition. However, in the 'play' condition, more of these conflicts and their resolutions were different from those in the original story and their stories were of higher quality (as measured by UK National Curriculum levels) than in the 'taught' condition. The analysis of the children's oral storytelling showed that in the 'play' condition, the children showed more confidence (measured on a 5-point scale from 'extremely unconfident and anxious' to 'extremely confident', based on observations of their behaviour) than in either of the other two conditions. This difference appears to have been mostly attributable to a greater number of children lacking confidence after the 'taught' condition. After the 'play condition', the children also showed more confidence in the oral storytelling activity than their teachers reported observing in their regular classroom activities.

A considerable proportion of the research related to children's pretence play, however, has investigated the benefits for social and emotional development of make-believe or socio-dramatic role play. Intriguingly, as Berk et al. (2006) review, while this kind of play is often characterised and perceived as 'free play', paradoxically it makes some of the greatest demands on children's self-restraint, or self-regulation. For, rather than following their own impulsive desires, they are obliged in this type of play to follow social rules. Given the importance of social competencies in human evolution noted in Chapter 3, it is perhaps not surprising that children throw themselves with such enthusiasm into a form of play which encourages and supports them to enact and acquire the rules of social life. Berk and colleagues report on a number of studies with 3- and 4-year-olds demonstrating a clear link between the complexity of socio-dramatic play and improvement in social responsibility. A further body of research has investigated the role of socio-dramatic play in the development of emotional self-regulation. Studies reported by Berk et al. (2006) have involved young children in coping with an experimenter induced, emotionally arousing make-believe event (a hungry crocodile puppet threatening to eat all the toys), and with the emotional stress of leaving their mother on the first day of pre-school. Such studies have shown how children learn to cope with such situations, and to develop improved levels of emotional regulation, through socio-dramatic play involving conflicts and their resolution. This type of work forms the foundation for therapeutic uses of play which, as Clark (2006) reviews, are both engaged in spontaneously by children in stressful or traumatic situations, and can be very productively facilitated and supported by adults in therapeutic contexts.

Two aspects of this kind of play which often concern practitioners or parents are play with imaginary friends and play with guns. However, the research evidence suggests that these are both quite normal and beneficial forms of imaginative play among young children and that attempts by adults to discourage or forbid them are generally counter-productive (i.e. the play persists but the relationship between the child and the adult is damaged). Studies of play with imaginary friends have shown that it has no effect on children's ability to distinguish fantasy from reality and children with imaginary friends typically have improved imagination and narrative skills (Taylor and Mannering 2006). Gun play, similar to rough-and-tumble, is easily distinguishable from real aggression or violence, in the same way that Tom and Jerry cartoons are easily distinguished from horror movies. In this kind of play, as in all other aspects of socio-dramatic play, children are developing their cooperative and social skills in contexts which are salient to their interests (see Holland, 2003, and Levin, 2006, for very useful insights in relation to this issue). Of course, because they are young children and developing their social skills and understandings, things sometimes go wrong, and pretend violence tips over into real violence (as rough-and-tumble can, occasionally and unfortunately, tip over into a real fight). The role of practitioners, clearly, is to help the children involved to learn to work through the problem when this happens, i.e. this kind of event can be most productively seen as an educational opportunity, rather than negatively as a reason to attempt to 'ban' this kind of play, which will inevitably be as hopeless as the attempt of myself and my wife to 'ban' Barbie dolls and 'My Little Ponies' – we finished up with bucket loads of them (see King Canute).

Socio-dramatic play is an area where there is a clear and important role for practitioners and other adults. First, in the provision of props – the golden rule here, as with choices about many toys, is that simple is best. Of course, a range of hats and costumes are useful, but basic dressing-up materials such as old sheets, bits of cloth, adult clothes which are past their best, etc. are much cheaper than ready-made costumes and can be used much more flexibly and imaginatively by young children. The same is true for a whole range of props – basic sticks, containers, cardboard boxes and general household items are much preferred to specially bought play equipment. There are just so many amazing things you can do with a washing machine box!

The second, and most important role for adults, however, is to get involved. Studies have clearly demonstrated the beneficial effects for the quality of children's pretend play of adult–child pretence, for example acting out a well-loved story together, and of adult modelling of pretence activities. For example, in one study with children aged between 27 and 41 months, after an adult acted out a sequence of pretence activities with dolls, the children's subsequent play with the dolls included many more imaginary acts, which were as likely to be novel as they were to be copies of the adult's activities

(Nielsen and Christie, 2008). We return to the general issues involved in adults' roles in children's play a little later in the chapter.

Games with rules

Finally, we come to playing games with rules. Observing children engaged in socio-dramatic play quickly teaches us that young children are strongly motivated by the need to make sense of their world and, as part of this, they are very interested in rules. However, this interest is far more generally manifested than just within socio-dramatic play. From a very young age, children begin to enjoy games with rules, and to invent their own. These include physical games such as chasing games, hide-and-seek, throwing and catching, etc. and, as children mature, more intellectual games such as board and card games, electronic and computer games, and the whole variety of sporting activities. In children from a very early age, a considerable proportion of time and energy playing any such game is devoted to establishing, agreeing, modifying and reminding one another about the rules.

As well as helping children to develop their understandings about rules, the main developmental contribution of playing games derives from their essentially social nature. While playing games with their friends, siblings and parents, young children are learning a range of social skills related to sharing, taking turns, understanding others' perspectives and so on. DeVries (2006) has usefully reviewed Piaget's significant contribution to the analysis of children's games for their social and moral development, together with subsequent research in this area.

The use of electronic and computer games (together with TV viewing) is a particular area of anxiety for parents. The concerns here relate to violence and to their lack of developmental or educational value. There is some evidence to suggest that excessive viewing of violent images can lead to increased aggression in children (although it is very difficult to establish the causal direction here, as children who show a lot of aggressive behaviour often enjoy watching and seek out portrayals of violence in the various media). Studies have also shown, however, that well-designed computer games can offer very engaging, creative, open-ended or problem-solving challenges to children, which are likely to share some of the benefits of problem solving or constructional play with objects. It is also the case that, despite worries about the solitary nature of electronic and computer games, in practice children enjoy these most when they are played with others and the best games stimulate a good deal of talk between children which helps develop their language skills (see Siraj-Blatchford and Whitebread, 2003, for a useful review of the benefits of computer and other ICT-based play in the early years).

The key point about games with rules, however, is that for young children this is an essentially social activity. Practitioners and other adults can very beneficially play games with children, and provide opportunities for children to play games with their peers.

The Role of Adults in Supporting Children's Play

While, of its essence, play is an area of activity that must be initiated and control-led by the child, it is nevertheless the case that adults are often involved in a variety of ways, and there is much that practitioners can do to enhance the edu-cational and developmental benefits of play for young children. Extensive research, some of which I have referred to above, has documented the role of parents (particularly mothers) in enhancing the quality of children's play through various kinds of involvement, including modelling play behaviours, providing useful resources, taking on a role in a playful scenario, and so on. Essentially, there seem to be four useful types of involvement in which adults can be produc-tively engaged, as follows:

- *Creating a supportive environment*: children are most likely to engage in the most complex forms of play, involving risk and challenge, and so derive the most educational and developmental benefit, when they feel emotionally secure; we have discussed these issues earlier in Chapter 2.
- *Providing a range of opportunities*: as I have argued throughout this chapter, children benefit from experiencing a good mix of the various types of play; this involves providing appropriate equipment and materials, which inspire and support young children to engage in the various types; challenges arising from cultural or gender-based expectations can arise here in relation to some aspects of play, but can mostly be addressed by responding sensitively to children's interests and enthusiasms; one way of doing this is through structuring.
- *Structuring*: this is a term first coined by Manning and Sharp (1977) and refers to the idea of developing playful projects in which the practitioner responds to the children's interests and provides opportunities for various types of play incorporated within a developing meaningful or narrative context; Drake (2009) provides many inspiring examples involving well-loved stories, children's interests (caring for animals – a lion comes to live in the classroom), problems to be solved and so on.
- *Participating*: it is well established that, if adults are able to play alongside children (such as playing with Play-Doh) or take on a role (such as a customer in the hairdressers'), this can enormously enhance the quality of the play, the language that it supports and so on; this requires great sensitivity – for example, it is far better to describe what you are doing than to ask the children what they are doing – but can be extremely productive (and informative about the children's real level of understanding).

While this all sounds perfectly straightforward when you write it down, however, it is clear that adult involvement in children's play, if it is to be productive, is not a simple matter and requires considerable skill. Fundamental to this, however, is a clear understanding of what children are learning through play and how the quality of their play experiences can be enhanced or undermined. I want to finish this chapter by referring to three current areas of research interest in this area which I believe are very helpful in this regard.

First, a series of studies by Howard and colleagues (see Howard, 2010), investigating young children's perceptions of play in their educational settings, has provided intriguing evidence of the hidden messages perceived by children and conveyed by practitioners about the nature of play. Children were shown in these studies to have quite different definitions of play to the adults in their settings, categorising activities as play or not play based on the amount of choice they offered, the apparent level of enjoyment of children involved in them, where they were located (floor = play; at a table = not play) and, in some settings, whether they involved books and whether an adult was present, both of which were taken as cues that the activity was not playful. Furthermore, these studies found that children engaged in activities they perceived as playful with increased enthusiasm and motivation, and produced a wider repertoire of problem-solving strategies (very much supporting Bruner's contention of play being crucially concerned with the development of cognitive flexibility). Performance on tasks presented to children in ways which they perceived as playful was significantly improved compared to that on the same tasks presented in ways which were not. This work clearly has powerful implications for practice, and clearly indicates that we need to be very mindful of the messages sent to children by the ways in which our early years settings are organised and how adults interact with them, particularly in playful contexts. It was notable, for example, that the impact of the adult present 'clue' was reduced or absent in settings where adults routinely and playfully engaged with the children in clearly playful activities.

Second, a number of researchers have begun to directly investigate the impact of adult involvement in children's play within educational settings. Principal among these has been Roberta Golinkoff and colleagues (see Singer et al., 2006) who have conducted and reviewed a number of studies examining the relative impact on the learning of vocabulary, concepts in shape and space, early numeracy and literacy and so on of various ways in which adults might involve themselves, or not, in children's play. This evidence, they have argued, strongly supports the notion of 'guided play' within educational contexts. Guided play, by their definition, involves two elements which appear to very largely support the other types of evidence we have reviewed so far. First, guided play involves a planned play environment, enriched with objects and toys which provide experiential learning opportunities and, second, it involves teachers participating in children's play by co-playing with them, asking open-ended questions and suggesting ways to explore materials that might not have been thought of by the children. In a typical experiment, for example, the aim was to teach 3–5-year-olds the concept of a triangle. The children were all taught that a triangle has three sides, but then experienced one of three conditions. One group experienced a guided play approach, which involved them in acting as detectives, alongside an adult, to discover the 'secret of the shapes'; the second group experienced a passive 'direct instruction' condition in which they watched an adult find the triangles; and the third group were given the same amount of time to engage in exploratory free play with the shapes. The guided learning group learnt to identify regular and irregular triangles significantly more reliably than children in either of the other groups. While these experimental studies appear to be rather directive in relation to the children's play (and reveal some of the difficulties of carrying out rigorous controlled research in this area), nevertheless they do illustrate that, certainly for some aspects of learning, children's play can be enhanced by sensitive adult involvement where the children's active playfulness is supported.

The third current area of research which I think is providing important insights into the nature of children's learning during play concerns the opportunities playful experiences provide for young children to develop their metacognitive and self-regulatory abilities. For example, we have referred to the research of Berk et al. (2006) earlier in relation to socio-dramatic play. As I have indicated throughout the book, this aspect of children's development in the early years is now widely recognised as being of fundamental significance. For this reason, the final chapter deals entirely with this topic. For now, however, it is worth noting that, as I argued in the first chapter of this book, and as I have argued elsewhere specifically in relation to play (Whitebread, 2010), children's self-regulatory development will be immeasurably enhanced in contexts where they experience emotional warmth and security and feelings of control, where they experience appropriate levels of cognitive challenge and ample opportunities to speak and reflect about their own learning. Playful contexts, sensitively supported by adults who are clear about their purposes and role, are powerfully and perhaps uniquely suited to providing these conditions in which young children thrive.

SUMMARY

I have placed this chapter in the centre of the book because this seems like the rightful place for a chapter on play in a book concerned with children's learning and development. As we have seen, it is ubiquitous in the activity and behaviour of young children and there is strong reason to believe that this is a consequence of evolutionary adaptation in humans, to enable us to develop the intellectual, emotional and social capabilities to respond to novel situations and problems. In our currently rapidly changing world, the importance of opportunities for playful learning for our young children would seem to be increasingly critical. Play is difficult to define and has proved challenging for researchers. However, I would want to argue that there are clear guidelines for early years practitioners emerging from the current resurgence of research in this area. To begin with, the issues raised in the previous chapters, concerned with emotional and social development, are

(Continued)

(Continued)

clearly inextricably linked to issues related to supporting children's play. However, some further points arise, as follows:

- There are many different forms of play, which can be categorised according to their developmental purposes into five broad types; provision needs to be made to support each of these types in as many forms as possible and to ensure that each child has a rich mixture of play experiences of all types.
- High-quality play is essentially initiated by the child and involves high levels of activity and engagement; children often set themselves challenges in play and reveal their real levels of understanding and ability; careful observation of children's play can, therefore, be a powerful – and the most valid – method of assessment.
- Careful observation of children's play must also be the basis for provision; practitioners can productively 'structure' play opportunities by providing problems, challenges, new materials, engaging narratives and so on, but this will only be successful if it is based on a sensitive response to children's interests.
- The production of private speech, including fantasy speech, by young children in playful contexts, indicates the challenging nature of the play for the child; as such, it is indicative of a high-quality play experience, and is also an important means by which children learn to internally represent their experiences and ideas in thought; practitioners can enhance and support this aspect of development by talking to the children during play, describing the nature of the experience, how it relates to other current and recent experiences, and so on.
- Practitioners can powerfully enhance the quality of children's play by participating; play should not be opposed to 'work', where the former is allowed when the latter has been completed; nor should play be something that is done by the children on their own and 'work' be something that is done with an adult or practitioner.
- Involvement of practitioners in children's playful activities will be most effective when the children retain control; only in this way can play experiences support children's developing self-regulation.

QUESTIONS FOR DISCUSSION

- Up to what age is it appropriate for children to play in school?
- Should we allow children to always have free choice in their play activities?
- What do we do about the child who always wants to play in the same way, or in the same area?
- Does adult play serve any useful purpose? Do we ever stop playing?

ACTIVITIES

A. Play observation

Carry out an observation of an individual child, or a group of children, engaged in self-initiated play for a period of 15–20 minutes. While you are observing, bear in mind the following questions:

1. What kinds of play are the children engaged in?

   Physical; play with objects; symbolic; pretence/socio-dramatic; games with rules? (Remember that more than one kind of play may be interwoven within one activity.)

2. What evidence is there that the children are actively engaged?

   (Think about involvement, concentration, mood, level of activity, effort, perseverance.)

3. To what extent is the children's play a social activity?

   a. Is there onlooking, parallel play, copying?
   b. Is there interaction?
   c. Are there disputes and how are these resolved?
   d. Is there cooperation?
   e. Is there role taking?

4. Do the children talk while they are playing? What kind of talk is it?

   a. To themselves or to others?
   b. Related to play activity or not?
   c. Describing/accompanying what is happening?
   d. Deciding what they need to do?
   e. Negotiating involvement with others?
   f. Deciding rules for the play?
   g. Playing a part or parts in a pretence?

5. What kind of enjoyment or satisfaction were the children deriving from the play?

   a. Sensory/physical?
   b. Cognitive/problem solving?
   c. Social/emotional/friendship?
   d. Personal achievement?

6. What, if anything, do you think the children might have been learning during this play activity?

B. Participation in play

You should also try to participate in the children's play in some way. How you do this will depend upon the age of the children and the kind of play they are engaged in. Here are some possibilities:

- playing alongside children in the sandpit, or with the lego/bricks, etc.
- taking on a role in fantasy play (having your hair cut in the hairdressers', visiting the king in his castle, being a patient in the hospital)
- making your own painting or model in the art area
- dancing with the children; making up a dance
- joining in skipping or other games in the playground
- playing a board, card or computer game with a group; making up a new board or card game
- making up a song/instrumental piece with a group
- swapping jokes with a group of children (or making a joke book!)
- making up a story or drama with a group of children (perhaps based on a story they choose) in which you maybe take a part.

When you participate, it is important that you don't dominate or take over in any way; your role is as a facilitator; avoid the temptation of trying to teach the children anything; let yourself be guided by them, and let them make all the decisions. Just let yourself play and have fun – this is important – children know if you are not genuine. After the event, try to answer the following questions:

- Did you facilitate the children's play: in what ways and by what means?
    a. Providing resources?
    b. Suggesting/modelling ideas?
    c. Helping them to resolve disputes?

- Was the children's play changed in any way by your presence?
  (Is there any evidence that the quality of the play and the children's involvement were enhanced or damaged?)

- Were you the centre of attention or just one of the group?
  (What were the consequences of this? Why/how did this happen?)

- Were the children pleased with your involvement?
  (Did they invite you to play again? Did other groups seek your involvement?)

- Did the children talk to you about the task/game or about other things?
  (There are issues here about the quality/structure of the play/game and about of talk other things related to building relationships/trust.)

- What did you learn about the children?
  (Abilities/understandings/interests/feelings/concerns/relationships – did you learn things that might not have been evident except in the play context?)

References

Bennett, N., Wood, L. and Rogers, S. (1997) *Teaching through Play*. Buckingham: Open University Press.

Berk, L.E., Mann, T.D. and Ogan, A.T. (2006) 'Make-believe play: wellspring for development of self-regulation', in D.G. Singer, R.M. Golinkoff and K. Hirsh-Pasek (eds) *Play = Learning: How Play Motivates and Enhances Children's Cognitive and Social–Emotional Growth* (pp. 74–100). Oxford: Oxford University Press.

Bornstein, M.H. (2006) 'On the significance of social relationships in the development of children's earliest symbolic play: an ecological perspective', in A. Göncü and S. Gaskins (eds) *Play and Development: Evolutionary, Sociocultural and Functional Perspectives* (pp. 101–29). Mahwah, NJ: Lawrence Erlbaum.

Bruner, J.S. (1972) 'Nature and uses of immaturity', *American Psychologist*, 27, 687–708.

Christie, J.F. and Roskos, K.A. (2006) 'Standards, science and the role of play in early literacy education', in D.G. Singer, R.M. Golinkoff and K. Hirsh-Pasek (eds) *Play = Learning*, Oxford: Oxford University Press.

Clark, C.D. (2006) 'Therapeutic advantages of play', in A. Göncü and S. Gaskins (eds) *Play and Development: Evolutionary, Sociocultural and Functional Perspectives* (pp. 275–93). Mahwah, NJ: Lawrence Erlbaum.

Cox, M. (1992) *Children's Drawings*. London: Penguin.

De Vries, R. (2006) 'Games with rules', in D. P. Fromberg and D. Bergen (eds) *Play from Birth to Twelve,* 2nd edn. Abingdon: Routledge.

Drake, J. (2009) *Planning for Children's Play and Learning*, 3rd edn. Abingdon: Routledge.

Frost, J.L. (2010) *A History of Children's Play and Play Environments: Toward a Contemporary Child-saving Movement*. London: Routledge.

Gaskins, S. (2000) 'Children's daily activities in a Mayan village: a culturally grounded description', *Journal of Cross-Cultural Research*, 34, 375–89.

Goldschmeid, E. and Jackson, S. (2003) *People Under Three: Young Children in Day Care,* 2nd edn. London: Routledge.

Guha, M. (1987) 'Play in School', in G.M. Blenkin and A.V. Kelly (eds) *Early Childhood Education* (pp. 61–79). London: Paul Chapman.

Holland, P. (2003) *We Don't Play With Guns Here.* Maidenhead: Open University Press.

Howard, J. (2010) 'Making the most of play in the early years: the importance of children's perceptions', in P. Broadhead, J. Howard and E. Wood (eds) *Play and Learning in the Early Years*. London: Sage.

Huleatt, H., Bruce, T., McNair, L. and Siencyn, S.W. (2008) *I Made a Unicorn! Open-ended Play with Blocks and Simple Materials*. Robertsbridge, East Sussex: Community Playthings (www.communityplaythings.co.uk).

Jarvis, P. (2010) '"Born to play": the biocultural roots of rough and tumble play, and its impact upon young children's learning and development', in P. Broadhead, J. Howard and E. Wood (eds) *Play and Learning in the Early Years*. London: Sage.

Karpov, Y.V. (2005) *The Neo-Vygotskian Approach to Child Development*. Cambridge: Cambridge University Press.

Levin, D.E. (2006) 'Play and violence: understanding and responding effectively', in D.P. Fromberg and D. Bergen (eds) *Play From Birth to Twelve: Context, Perspectives, and Meanings,* 2nd edn (pp. 395–404). London: Routledge.

Malloch, S. and Trevarthen, C. (2009) *Communicative Musicality: Exploring the Basis of Human Companionship*. Oxford: Oxford University Press.

Manning, K. and Sharp, A. (1977) *Structuring Play in the Early Years at School*. Cardiff: Ward Lock Educational.

Moyles, J. (1989) *Just Playing? The Role and Status of Play in Early Childhood Education.* Milton Keynes: Open University Press.

Nielsen, M. and Christie, T. (2008) 'Adult modeling facilitates young children's generation of novel pretend acts', *Infant and Child Development,* 17(2), 151–62.

Pellegrini, A.D. (2009) *The Role of Play in Human Development*. Oxford: Oxford University Press.

Pellegrini, A.D. and Gustafson, K. (2005) 'Boys' and girls' uses of objects for exploration, play and tools in early childhood', in A.D. Pellegrini and P.K. Smith (eds) *The Nature of Play: Great Apes and Humans* (pp. 113–35). New York: Guilford Press.

Pellegrini, A.D. and Smith, P.K. (1998) 'Physical activity play: the nature and function of a neglected aspect of play', *Child Development,* 69(3), 577–98.

Pellis, S. and Pellis, V. (2009) *The Playful Brain*. Oxford: Oneworld Publications.

Piaget, J. (1959) *The Language and Thought of the Child*. London: Routledge and Kegan Paul.

Pound, L. (2010) 'Playing music', in J. Moyles (ed.). *The Excellence of Play*. Maidenhead: Open University Press.

Power, T.G. (2000) *Play and Exploration in Children and Animals.* Mahwah, NJ: Lawrence Erlbaum.

Ring, K. (2010) 'Supporting a playful approach to drawing', in P. Broadhead, J. Howard and E. Wood (eds) *Play and Learning in the Early Years.* London: Sage.

Singer, D.G., Golinkoff, R.M. and Hirsh-Pasek, K. (2006) *Play = Learning: How Play Motivates and Enhances Children's Cognitive and Social-emotional Growth.* Oxford: Oxford University Press.

Siraj-Blatchford, J. and Whitebread, D. (2003) *Supporting Information and Communication Technology in the Early Years.* Buckingham: Open University Press.

Smith,P.K. (1990) 'The role of play in the nursery and primary school curriculum', in C. Rogers, and P. Kutnick (eds) *The Social Psychology of the Primary School* (pp. 144–168). London: Routledge.

Smith, P.K. (2006) 'Evolutionary foundations and functions of play: an overview', in A. Göncü and S. Gaskins (eds) *Play and Development: Evolutionary, Sociocultural and Functional Perspectives* (pp. 21–49). Mahwah, NJ: Lawrence Erlbaum.

Smith, P.K. (2010) *Children and Play.* Chichester: Wiley-Blackwell.

Sylva, K. and Czerniewska, P. (1985) *Play: Personality, Development and Learning (Unit 6, E206).* Milton Keynes: Open University Press.

Sylva, K., Bruner, J.S. and Genova, P. (1976) 'The role of play in the problem-solving of children 3–5 years old', in J.S. Bruner, A. Jolly and K. Sylva (eds) *Play: Its Role in Development and Evolution* (pp. 55–67). London: Penguin.

Tamis-LeMonda,C.S. and Bornstein, M.H. (1989) 'Habituation and maternal encourage-ment of attention in infancy as predictors of toddler language, play and representa-tional competence', *Child Development*, 60, 738–51.

Taylor, M. and Mannering, A.M. (2006) 'Of Hobbes and Harvey: the imaginary com-panions created by children and adults', in A. Göncü and S. Gaskins (eds), *Play and Development: Evolutionary, Sociocultural and Functional Perspectives* (pp. 227–45). Mahwah, NJ: Lawrence Erlbaum.

Thomas, G.V. and Silk, A.M.J. (1990) *An Introduction to the Psychology of Children's Drawings.* Hemel Hempstead: Harvester Wheatsheaf.

Tovey, H. (2007) *Playing Outdoors: Spaces and Places, Risk and Challenge.* Maidenhead: Open University Press.

Trevarthen, C. (1999) 'Musicality and the intrinsic motive pulse: evidence from human psychobiology and infant communication', in *Rhythms, Musial Narrative, and the Origins of Human Communication. Musicae Scientiae,* Special Issue, 1999–2000 (pp. 157–213). Liege: European Society for the Cognitive Sciences of Music.

Vygotsky, L.S. (1978) 'The role of play in development', in *Mind in Society* (pp. 92–104). Cambridge, MA: Harvard University Press.

Vygotsky, L. (1986) *Thought and Language.* Cambridge, MA: MIT Press.

Whitebread, D. (2010) 'Play, metacognition and self-regulation', in P. Broadhead, J. Howard and E. Wood (eds) *Play and Learning in the Early Years.* London: Sage.

Whitebread, D. and Jameson, H. (2010) 'Play beyond the Foundation Stage: story-telling, creative writing and self-regulation in able 6–7 year olds', in J. Moyles (ed.) *The Excellence of Play,* 3rd edn (pp. 95–107). Maidenhead: Open University Press.

Chapter 5

Memory and Understanding

Key Questions

- How does our memory work?
- What memory abilities are present in very young children?
- In what ways do memory abilities develop?
- How does memory relate to learning and understanding?
- How can we help children to develop effective memory abilities?

Learning, Remembering and Early Years Education

In this chapter and the next, we move on to the more cognitive aspects of children's development. Of course, these are intrinsically bound up with and interdependent upon the more emotional and social aspects of development with which we have concerned ourselves in the earlier chapters. It is also the case that, within cognitive development itself, there are multiple interdependent systems which are not easily pulled apart for separate consideration. The processes of learning, thinking, understanding, remembering, problem solving and so on are very much related to each other, and on a moment-by-moment basis. However, for the purposes of discussion and elucidation, we are obliged to make these distinctions. The present chapter, therefore, focuses on those aspects of cognitive development which developmental psychology has generally explored in the context of memory, and the next focuses on those concerned with learning.

The development of memory abilities in young children is yet another area in which research has made significant discoveries in the last 20 years or so. As is so often the case in science (think of telescopes in astronomy), these discoveries have been made largely due to the introduction of new methodologies. The use of mostly verbal recall methods in memory research in the past led to the view, now recognised as being completely erroneous, that, before the age of around 3 years, young children lived almost entirely in the 'here and now' and were not capable of forming mental representations of the past. As a consequence, their memories were thought to be limited and unorganised. New eye-tracking technologies, however, have allowed the development of methodologies which use pre-verbal infants' eye gaze to examine the extent to which they remember and recognise objects, pictures, faces and so on. For example, infants as young as 5 months old, if shown a face they have seen before (up to 2 weeks previously!) and a face they have not seen, will look much more at the familiar than the unfamiliar face. Simple observation has also shown that, by 17 months old, in contexts with which they are familiar, children can reliably remember a sequence of activities (such as those involved in giving a teddy a bath) and reproduce them. Patricia Bauer (2002) has written an excellent introduction to this new work, and has conducted much of it herself and with colleagues at the University of Minnesota. An important outcome of this recent work, Bauer and others have concluded, is a new recognition that 'infant amnesia', or our inability to recall events in our lives before the age of around 3–4 years, is more a consequence of the limitations of early verbal abilities than it is a reflection of the limitations of early memory.

While some aspects of our memory abilities seem to be in place from very early infancy, however, there are other aspects in which there is very clear development. Indeed, it is one of the many fascinations and challenges of teaching young children that they not only have much to learn, but also much to learn about learning itself. The early years practitioner cannot simply place the material to be learnt, remembered or understood in front of the children and let them get on with it. If this were the case, early years teaching would be very straightforward and probably extremely dull.

This distinction between different aspect or types of remembering and learning is evidenced by the common observation that children appear to learn very effectively before they arrive at school and before anyone starts trying to teach them anything, but then often encounter difficulties in learning in school. Amongst many other accomplishments, before they arrive in school, in the first few years of life, the vast majority of children achieve the astonishing feat of learning to speak a language, and sometimes two. It is only in school that significant numbers of children begin to find learning and remembering difficult. The learning they are required to do in school, however, is distinctive and more challenging in two important ways:

- It requires them to deliberately and explicitly memorise information of various kinds, much of it arbitrary (letters of the alphabet, phoneme–grapheme correspondences, written numbers) or unrelated to their everyday world (Tudors and Stuarts, the properties of a triangle, energy and forces).

- It requires them to understand and develop ideas and concepts which are part of a planned and delivered 'curriculum' rather than arising naturally from their life experiences.

Of course, this is less the case in the early years of schooling, but increasingly so as children proceed through the education system. In a sense, in the early years, therefore, we are engaged in helping children to make the transition from 'incidental' to 'deliberate' remembering and learning. This transition is not just a requirement of schooling, however, but is, from a developmental psychological point of view, a crucial part of children's development of cognitive self-awareness and control. As such, it facilitates the development of the whole range of higher mental processes involved in reasoning, thinking, problem solving, decision making, and so on. The challenge for the early years educator, therefore, is to devise activities and experiences which will present ideas and information to children in ways which are memorable, which make it easy for them to understand, but at the same time help children to develop their memory and learning capabilities; or, in other words, help them to become increasingly independent, self-regulated learners.

An understanding of the ways in which children's memory and learning capabilities develop is clearly fundamental to devising such activities and experiences. The aim of this chapter, therefore, is to set out what psychologists currently understand about the structure and development of human memory and its role in the ways in which children learn and make sense of their world. As we shall see, recent research by neuroscientists on the workings of the brain has combined with insights from cognitive developmental psychology to provide some very clear guidelines which, properly applied in the hands of a skilled teacher, can transform the effectiveness of attempts to teach young children, and help them to become effective learners.

The Structure of the Human Memory System

Research on memory has shown it to be a complex and multi-faceted aspect of human cognitive processing. We do not have a memory so much as several memory systems, each with its own structural characteristics which fit it to performing a different function. This aspect of human memory can easily be demonstrated by considering the things which we find easy and difficult to remember. To illustrate this, before reading any further, write down which of the following you find easiest to remember, and which you find most difficult:

- the melodies of songs
- the letters of the alphabet
- how to ride a bicycle
- the names of people you meet
- lecture notes

- the 50 states of America
- telephone numbers
- how to draw a face
- what happened at an important interview
- where your keys are when you have lost them
- the colours of the rainbow
- new information about something in which you are interested
- important information about something uninteresting.

If you try this activity with a group of adults, typically there are areas of agreement and disagreement. That some people can remember melodies but not numbers, while others can remember telephone numbers but not people's names, suggests very strongly that there are separate systems for the different types of information. In the same way, some people have strong visual memories, while others can remember information expressed verbally much more efficiently.

In other areas, there is usually almost unanimous agreement. Practical memories like how to ride a bike and draw a face are unproblematic. The letters of the alphabet and colours of the rainbow have been made secure through a combination of repetition, song and mnemonics. We would recognise the 50 states of America even if we couldn't actually recall them all. We know how to work out where our keys are by 'rewinding' our internal videotape of our recent experiences. What happened at an interview and new information related to an interest seem to stick, while lecture notes and information about things which don't interest us just disappear into the ether. I have looked at lecture notes I have written, sometimes fairly recently, and have no recollection of them at all – although the interesting new idea they included might by now be a central part of my thinking.

All this is a testament to the complex but very particular ways in which the human memory system works and its impact on our learning. It is a system perfectly adapted to perform certain kinds of memory and learning tasks highly efficiently; in order to do this, for example, it has developed the ability to discard unimportant information as efficiently as it remembers what is important.

The seminal work in analysing the structure of the human memory system was the 'multistore' model proposed by Atkinson and Shiffrin (1968). They proposed that there are essentially three different kinds of memory store, namely Sensory, Short-term and Long-term. This model was supported at the time by detailed research evidence and much of the subsequent work in this area has simply developed this basic model in more detail. Figure 5.1 sets out diagrammatically what is broadly the current consensus model of the various structures and processes in human memory. We will refer to this model throughout the chapter. In the remainder of the chapter, research related to each part of the human memory system and its development will be reviewed and major implications for early years pedagogy revealed.

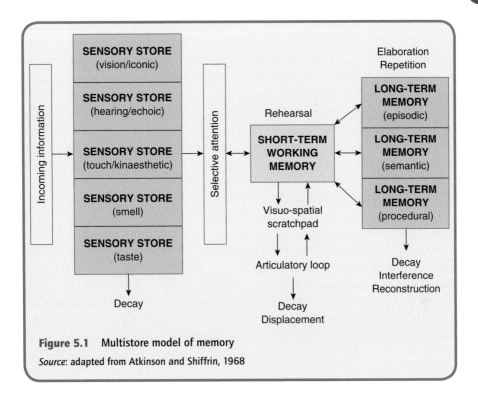

Figure 5.1 Multistore model of memory

Source: adapted from Atkinson and Shiffrin, 1968

Sensory Stores, Recognition and Selective Attention

According to this model, incoming information from the environment is first received via the various sensory receptors into the sensory stores (one for each sense modality). These appear to operate as an initial screening device which holds information just long enough (approximately half a second) for the important, significant or relevant information to be sorted out from the rest and transferred to the short-term store (or working memory, as it is now called). The trace of the overwhelming majority of the information which is not selected rapidly decays and is lost.

An example of how this works is the classic 'cocktail party' experiment where you are in a crowded room, listening intently to the conversation in your group and filtering out the rest, until someone on the other side of the room says your name. Immediately, your attention switches to the other conversation. This demonstrates two important features of our memory system: the primacy of 'recognition' and the power of 'selective attention'.

Recognition

Although we are not aware of it, we are continuously monitoring all the information coming in to our sensory receptors. This process of monitoring involves the earliest and simplest form of memory, namely recognition. The human brain is astonishingly good at recognising information it has already attended to and received on a previous occasion. Recent work by neuroscientists has revealed that knowledge is stored in the brain as patterns of links between neurones, or brain cells. Learning is thus a process of establishing patterns, pattern matching and making links between patterns. When some information we have already encountered before is received again, it excites an already established pattern of neurones, and this exact match is perceived as recognition. As this is fundamental to the way our long-term memory system works, it is an ability with which we are born. Experiments with very young children have shown that their pure recognition memories are equal to those of adults (as anyone who has lost to very young children playing the 'find the pairs' card game will attest!).

This neurological work explains why we can always recognise information more easily than we can recall it. For example, we will reliably recognise someone's face, but recalling their name may be more difficult. Recognition simply requires that the incoming pattern of sensory information be matched. Recall, however, requires us to do this and then to find a linked pattern. As we shall see later, the strength of the links between different neuronal patterns depends upon repetition. At this point, however, it is most important to note that our attention is largely guided by the recognition process.

Selective attention

This leads on to the second point, that the 'cocktail' party phenomenon also demonstrates the power of selective attention. A situation which all too often arises at parties is where you are politely listening to someone droning on about something which you find completely boring. Meanwhile, the people in the next group are talking excitedly about your favourite film, sharing some juicy gossip about someone you know, or having an uproarious time telling one another what are obviously some extremely funny jokes. Maintaining attention on the conversation about your companion's plumbing problems, or which route they took to the party, becomes quite impossible.

The early years classroom, of course, shares certain characteristics with a crowded party and there are many opportunities for children to be distracted. Whereas an adult might be capable of forcing themselves to attend to one element of their current sensory input rather than another, young children have not yet learnt this control. Hagen and Hale (1973) demonstrated the development of selective attention by asking 5–6-year-olds and 14–15-year-olds to remember pictures on a series of cards. Each card actually contained two pictures, but one of the pictures was identified as the important one to be remembered. In these circumstances, the 14–15-year-olds remembered many more of the important pictures than the 5–6-year-olds; however, the younger children remembered many more of the pictures they were not asked to remember. So the total amount of information remembered was the same for both groups of children, but the older group focused their attention much more effectively.

Recognition of the powerful and active nature of our selective attention makes it very clear why it is vital that activities intended to help young children learn must first and foremost interest them, intrigue them and be personally relevant for them. Only then can their attention be held, because they have not yet learnt to exercise deliberate control very effectively.

Importantly, grabbing young children's attention will involve a strong element of recognition, together with the promise of new information related to what they already know. If it does not, attention will be easily diverted and all the important information the adult practitioner has carefully planned and prepared will be discarded from their sensory stores within 0.5 seconds.

Sensory channels

A separate but equally important characteristic of the sensory stores mechanism is that each seems to be a unitary channel capable of passing on just one item of information at a time. As a consequence, different pieces of information coming in through the same sense modality tend to interfere with one another. It is, therefore, impossible to listen to two people talking at once, even if they are both trying to tell you the same thing. Related pieces of information coming in through different modalities (such as sound and vision), on the other hand, tend to support and reinforce one another.

When new information, ideas or concepts are being introduced to young children, enlisting the power of this multi-sensory message support is vital. Young children find it particularly difficult to acquire knowledge simply through listening to talk or reading text. The power of illustrations in young children's picture books and information books is a testament to this. Particularly when they are being introduced to something new, they need to see and hear, touch and physically experience it in as numerous a variety of ways as possible. A multi-sensory approach to activities designed to help children's learning is always likely to be most successful. This is why the sensory richness of first-hand experiences will always help children's learning.

As we shall see, sense specific processes and representations are also an important element in both short- and long-term memory.

Short-term store and working memory

The central structure of the human memory system identified by Atkinson and Shiffrin was the short-term store. Subsequent work by Baddeley and Hitch (1974), however, redescribed this as working memory, which is the usual term now used. The point here is that this aspect of the memory system can be more accurately characterised as a set of dynamic processes, rather than as a static store.

Importantly, the working memory is where we bring information into consciousness so that we can work on it. It has three distinctive features which have major significance for children's abilities to carry out a wide range of cognitive tasks and which determine the ways in which memory develops.

Rehearsal and the articulatory loop

The first distinctive feature of the short-term store or working memory system is that information held here, as with the sensory stores, is also subject to decay. However, the process of decay here is rather slower. Whereas information is lost after half a second from the sensory stores, research indicates that information lasts about half a minute in the working memory. Furthermore, if information is needed longer than this, it can be restored afresh by the process of 'rehearsal'. It is as though information in working memory is travelling along a conveyor belt. The journey from one end to the other lasts 30 seconds, after which items fall off the end and are lost. However, it is possible to pick up items just before they fall and place them back on the beginning of the conveyor again, giving them another 30 seconds. This re-inputting of items of information can be done repeatedly.

As well as allowing information to be held in memory for as long as we need to use it, rehearsal has also been shown to serve another purpose, which is the transfer of information from short-term to long-term memory. A range of evidence has demonstrated that the more information is rehearsed, the longer-lasting it will be. For example, a well-established pattern in list learning experiments is that the first few items on a list are recalled better than items later on. This is known as the 'primacy effect'. If more rehearsal is allowed by, for example, slowing down the speed at which the list is presented, then the primacy effect is increased. On the other hand, if the opportunity for rehearsal is removed by, for example, requiring subjects to engage in the 'distractor task' of counting backwards between the presentation of the words in the list, then the primacy effect disappears.

The central role of rehearsal in both holding information in working memory and transferring items to long-term memory has enormous educational implications. This is particularly the case because of evidence that the use of rehearsal itself develops through the early years and primary school age range. In a very influential series of experiments, Flavell et al. (1966) revealed that, in a short-term memory task, the percentage of children spontaneously using rehearsal grew from 10% of 5-year-olds to 60% of 7-year-olds and 85% of 10-year-olds. Not only the quantity, but also the quality of rehearsal develops, with older children and college students using more sophisticated, cumulative and flexible patterns of repetition in their rehearsal strategies.

In the working memory model, which Baddeley (1986, 2006) and many others have continued to work on and develop, the process of rehearsal is reconfigured as the 'articulatory or phonological loop'. This title recognises more recent evidence that conscious rehearsal is a process specific to verbal information, and that it involves articulation by an 'inner voice'. Detailed research has linked the development of an effective articulatory or phonological loop with reading fluency; among this is clear evidence that children with developmental dyslexia have greatly reduced memory spans.

Multi-sensory representations

Second, the multi-sensory nature of short-term memory must also be acknowledged. We are all aware, for example, of our ability to hold visual images in our minds and this has been recognised in more recent versions of the working memory model (Baddeley, 1986, 2006) with the inclusion of a second system referred to as the 'visuo-spatial scratch pad'. This system allows the storage of a visual image which can be manipulated to carry out tasks. Just as the reception of information through more than one sensory modality appears to powerfully reinforce the message initially, its representation in more than one sense modality in working memory appears to dramatically increase its memorability. Teaching strategies and practices which encourage children to form and use visual images as representations of their understandings, particularly in areas such as mathematics and problem solving, have been shown to be highly beneficial.

Limited capacity

Third, the working memory system has limited capacity. In a very early and seminal article, Miller (1956) reviewed evidence that the adult human can usually hold around seven pieces of information in short-term memory. As new pieces of information enter, either from current sensory inputs or retrieved from long-term memory, some existing pieces of information are displaced. This can easily be demonstrated. Try the following letter translation task. For each item, there are some letters and a number. Having looked at each item, you must shut your eyes while you start with each letter in turn and count on the number of letters through the alphabet, so that you produce a new list of letters. When you have the new list formed in your mind, you open your eyes and write them down. Keep going until it becomes impossible:

A + 6
B K + 4
M J C + 5
K S D P + 3
R L T E N + 4
F O H Q G I + 2

It has long been established that young children appear to have a smaller working memory capacity than adults. Dempster (1981), for example, investigated how many randomly selected numbers or letters children of different ages and adults could remember and found a clear developmental sequence, as illustrated in Figure 5.2.

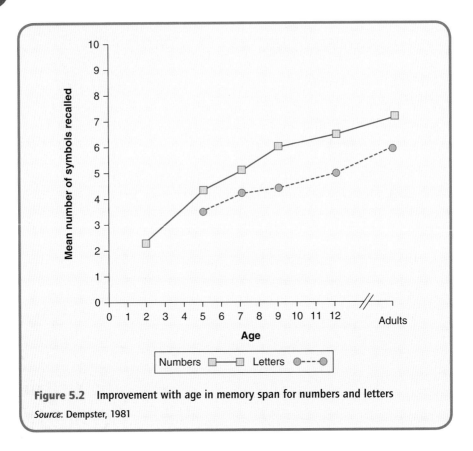

Figure 5.2   Improvement with age in memory span for numbers and letters

Source: Dempster, 1981

We will examine the causes of this developmental sequence below. For the moment, however, it is important to recognise how fundamental working memory is to a wide range of cognitive activity and that children may often have difficulty with tasks not through a failure of understanding, but because they cannot hold sufficient information in their mind. Thus, when young children are attempting to articulate their thoughts, or to read, or to carry out a numerical task, you will often experience them 'losing the thread' for this very reason.

In these circumstances, it is an important function of an adult to 'scaffold' the task for the child by providing support in the form of reminders of the vital pieces of information that have been displaced from the working memory. To understand the nature of the child's experience, it is perhaps helpful to remember the experience of learning to drive a car. To begin with, there is simply just too much to think about all at once. It is possible to change gear just so long as one is not required to steer at the same time. For young children in the early years of their education, this must be a very common state of affairs.

The mechanisms by which novice learners come to be able to cope with the large amounts of information involved in such complex tasks as articulating an argument, reading, solving a mathematical problem or driving a car turn out to have major pedagogical implications. To begin with, when faced with the data presented in Figure 5.2, psychologists advanced the view that children simply had smaller working memory capacities which gradually grew (like their arms and legs). However, subsequent work has shown that adults' apparently larger capacity is really a consequence of three aspects of development which allow them to use their fixed capacity more efficiently. The first of these relates to an increase in the speed and 'automatocity' with which memory processes, like every other aspect of brain functioning, can be executed by adults due to practice effects. As educators we can recognise this, but there is not much we can do to alter it. The other two, which are of much more interest to us as educators, relate to improvements in our knowledge base as we grow older and increasing self-awareness and control of our own cognitive processes.

Improved Knowledge Base

In a very elegant experiment, Chi (1978) demonstrated that it is knowledge rather than age which determines memory abilities in any particular area. She asked 10-year-olds and adults to recall lists of 10 digits, and to recall the positions of chess pieces on a chess board. As you would expect, the adults outperformed the children on digit recall, but, surprisingly, the tables were turned with the chess pieces. The result was explained, however, by the fact that the children were all regular chess players and the adults were not. It turns out that the improved knowledge base of the expert helps memory in a number of ways, and we will return to this when we look at long-term memory below. Chi's experiment, however, appears to illustrate the phenomenon of 'chunking'. This is the process by which, as we become more expert and knowledgeable in a particular area, we do not simply acquire more information, we also increasingly structure the information. Common structures, originally made up of lots of individual pieces of information, themselves become just one piece of information. This is illustrated by the following memory task. Try to remember each of the following sets of 12 numbers or letters. Look at each for 3 seconds, then cover them up and try to write them down.

1. 9 5 8 2 3 5 4 1 6 7 0 3
2. 1 0 6 6 1 9 4 5 2 0 0 1
3. 1 2 3 4 5 6 7 8 9 1 0 1
4. q g u d x v n y r p l a
5. c a t d o g l e g a r m
6. a b c d e f g h i j k l

Clearly, the sequences which contained structures with which you were already familiar are far easier to remember than those which do not, because you can remember the information in meaningful 'chunks' and this reduces the load on working memory. In Chi's experiment, similarly, the child chess players were able to remember structures of chess pieces in 'chunks'.

It is important to recognise that young children's relative lack of experience in most knowledge domains means that the vast majority of even apparently simple tasks will place a heavier load on their working memory capacity. This is one reason why children can often manage a new task, skill or strategy they have been taught, more easily when it is put in a familiar context.

Metacognitive Monitoring and Strategic Control

The ability to use our limited working memory capacity more and more efficiently is also achieved by our increasing self-awareness of our own memory abilities and the development and use of strategies based on this knowledge. This 'metacognitive' aspect of children's developing abilities to learn and carry out more sophisticated tasks was first identified by Flavell et al. (1966) in their explorations of rehearsal. They asked the question whether young children failed to rehearse because they were incapable of doing so, or because they were not aware this might be a useful strategy. So they used a simple memory task, involving sequences of pictures, and attempted to teach 5-year-olds to rehearse. As it turned out, these young children were perfectly capable of rehearsing, and performed as well as older children when they did so. However, when subsequently asked to carry out another such task, about half of them reverted to their original pattern of not rehearsing and failing to remember.

This early work has led to an emormous body of research concerned with the development of children's 'metamemory', or their increasing awareness of their own memory abilities, and its relation to the construction and use of increasingly sophisticated strategies. Children's lack of self-awareness has been well documented. For example, Wellman (1977) investigated the 'tip-of-the-tongue' phenomenon and showed that children's awareness of when they know something, but cannot currently recall it, is far less accurate than that of an adult. Istomina (1975) revealed young children's gradually emerging self-awareness in a memory task which consisted of a game within which the children had to go to a 'store' to buy an agreed list of five items for a pretend tea party. Valerik displayed the typical behaviour of a 3-year-old. When asked to go to the store:

> Valerik, obviously pleased with the proposition, turns his head immediately toward the store and takes the basket. 'OK,' he says, and runs off without waiting to hear the experimenter's last words.

> In the store, Valerik inspects all the wares on display with great curiosity. When the store manager (experimenter's assistant) asks him 'What have you been told to buy?' Valerik nods his head towards the toys and then says, 'Candy.'

> 'And what else?' says the manager.

> Valerik begins to glance about nervously and frowns ... 'Can I be the sales clerk?' he asks.

By 4 years old, however, some kinds of primitive strategy are beginning to emerge:

> Igor ... listens to the instructions patiently, attentively looking at the experimenter with an air of importance; he then runs off, forgetting even to take the basket with him. 'Give me noodles, a ball, butter, and that's all,' he says quickly ... 'And hurry, because the children are hungry.'

Igor's recognition of his need to listen with his full attention and then to rush to carry out the task demonstrates some awareness of his own memory abilities and limitations. It is not until 5 years old, however, that Istomina found children commonly beginning to rehearse and to be aware of any forgetting:

> Serezha listened attentively to the list and repeated each of the experimenter's words in a whisper. He recalls four items, but could not recall the fifth. He looked confusedly at the experimenter, and repeated the same words one more time. 'There's something else I have to buy, but I've forgotten it,' he said.

It is not, of course, until we become aware that we are failing to remember or to understand that we recognise the need to carry out a task differently. Self-monitoring of performance is thus fundamental to developing our ability to be more effective learners. The common experience of suddenly realising that you have been 'reading' a text but haven't taken in any of the meaning is a testimony to this. Has this happened to you so far in this chapter? Let's hope not too often. But if it did, I'm sure you would recognise it and do something about it.

As a consequence, encouraging children to self-monitor their performance on tasks can be enormously effective in developing their ability to learn. Children can be asked to predict how they are likely to do on a task. They can also be usefully taught strategies such as:

- rehearsal and cumulative rehearsal
- using visual imagery
- making arbirary information more meaningful so that it can be chunked, for example Richard Of York Gave Battle In Vain (colours of the rainbow); Big Elephants Can't Always Understand Small Elephants (how to spell 'because') and so on
- turning recall into recognition by generating possibilities, for example the alphabetic method
- thinking back to the context in which the to-be-remembered item was first encountered.

This is by no means an exhaustive list; the ingenuity with which the human brain constructs a wide range and variety of such strategies is astonishing. Each of these strategies depends for its success upon a structural feature of our memory systems. As children become more self-aware about their own memories and ways of learning, so they become more adept at generating their own strategies and matching them ever more appropriately to particular tasks. Nisbet and Shucksmith (1986), amongst others, have also shown that young children can be taught strategies and will adopt them if they are clearly associated with successful performance. Explicit discussion and modelling by an adult are effective means of encouraging children to try a wide range of memory strategies. There is also evidence that once children have used one strategy successfully, they are more likely to behave strategically on other occasions. It is by this means that the fundamentals of true independent, self-regulated learning would appear to be established.

In an important series of studies, Ornstein and colleagues (see Ornstein et al., 2010) have looked at teaching practices which seem to encourage and support the development by young children of improved memory abilities. In one study, for example, they demonstrated that the proportion of first grade teachers' talk which was 'memory relevant' was generally quite low, ranging from 0 to 12%. This talk included the suggestion of memory strategies and asking metacognitive questions, for example asking children to suggest possible strategies or asking them to justify their approach to trying to remember something. They also looked at the co-occurrence of this memory talk with memory demands (for example, reminding children about a recall strategy when they are asked to recall something). This was also a relatively infrequent practice, but varied considerably amongst the sample of teachers in the study. They discovered that both these variations, however, not only made a significant difference to the children's use of memory strategies at the time, with consequent improvements in performance, but that these differences were still present through to fourth grade.

This study, of course, was conducted with children at the top end of what we would generally regard as the early years of schooling (Grade 1 in the States would be Year 2 in the UK currently). However, we know from other studies, such as Istomina's, that children much younger than this are perfectly capable of carrying out simple memory strategies. The key point here is that there are important individual differences, with some children naturally developing strategies and some not (as we shall discuss further in Chapter 7). So, modelling, suggesting and supporting ways of remembering things, with children as young as 3 years, when they have something to remember (the procedure for doing a painting, where they have left something, what they need to bring to school tomorrow), can be of enormous benefit.

Long-term Memory

Atkinson and Shiffrin's original conception of a long-term store has also been refined and developed by subsequent research. The generally accepted current model is that originally proposed by Tulving (1985) who argued that long-term memory has, in fact, three distinct components: procedural, episodic and semantic memory. The evidence for this mainly arises from the study of amnesic patients who, in different circumstances and conditions, lose certain kinds of memories but not others.

These three different kinds of long-term memory depend on different kinds of representations and store different kinds of knowledge. Intriguingly, the forms of representations used appear to relate closely to those identified by the eminent developmental psychologist, Jerome Bruner (1974), in his very influential model of the development of learning. Bruner's model emphasises the role within intellectual development of the use of different modes of representation –

- 'enactive': memories of actions
- 'iconic': memories of unreconstructed perceptions: visual images/sounds/smells, etc.
- 'symbolic': memories of experience transformed into a symbolic code (language/mathematics etc): thoughts/ideas/concepts, etc.

Each of these modes is increasingly accessible to our conscious awareness and increasingly flexible. Thus, procedural memory relies on enactive representations, episodic memory on iconic (mainly visual) representations, and semantic memory on symbolic (mainly verbal) representations. The evidence from studies of the evolution of the human brain suggests that these modes of representation and their related memory systems emerged in this order (and, very broadly, are related to the three areas of the human brain indicated earlier in Figure 2.2 in the chapter on emotional development). Perhaps as a consequence, while there are complex interactions between them, the more primitive enactive/procedural and iconic/episodic memories seem to be able to support symbolic/semantic memory more than is the case the other way around.

Procedural memory

The procedural memory is the repository of our developing knowledge about how to carry out actions: for example, feed ourselves with a spoon, fasten a button, hop, ride a bicycle, write with a pencil, hit a ball. The memories or knowledge of how to do these things are stored enactively and are not accessible to conscious verbalisations.

It is, of course, possible to describe our physical actions in language, but doing so does not seem to help improve their quality or efficiency very much, if at all. I have, for example, read countless descriptions of the perfect golf swing, but the way I have improved my own performance is through practice; when I hit a great shot is when I remember how a good swing feels physically, not how to describe it verbally.

Conversely, there is some evidence to suggest that encoding verbal information enactively can be a very powerful mnemonic. Spelling, it has been claimed by some, is 'in the hand', and it is a commonly reported experience that when we have forgotten momentarily how to spell a word (i.e. cannot access our symbolic representation of it), it helps to write it out by hand. Certainly, there is good evidence that linking new information to actions for children can be very helpful: for example, making the patterns of letters and numbers with whole arm movements in the air, or in sand, or linking new words or songs to be remembered to sequences of actions.

Episodic memory

Episodic memory appears to be a system whereby an initially quite detailed record is kept of our experiences. Although the most significant of these is probably the visual record, it includes information from all the sensory inputs. It is indicative of the way in which these memories are recorded that we have to run through them in the sequence in which they originally occurred in order to locate any particular memory. For example, if we have misplaced our keys/glasses/wallet or whatever, it is possible and often very effective to 'rerun' our memories of the day so far, starting at the point where we have a definite memory of the lost item. It is as though we can rerun a kind of videotape of our experiences in our head.

While the rather fixed and 'iconic' nature of the memories within episodic memory have their limitations, this is nevertheless a very powerful aspect of human long-term memory. Research has shown that everything we learn, even as adults, is initially most strongly linked to the particular context and sequence of events in which we first experienced it (see, for example, Conway et al., 1997). It is also a common experience that revisiting somewhere we have not been for a long time, or coming across a particular smell or sound, will trigger memories of particular events which were originally associated with them (and which we often had previously not recalled).

Reminding ourselves of the context in which something was originally learnt or encountered is consequently often one of the most effective ways of recalling information, and this is a technique we can teach to children. We can also make use of the power of episodic memory in other ways. It is no accident that important cultural information is mainly transmitted in pre-literate cultures by means of stories, myths and legends. As experienced practitioners are well aware, for young children also, setting new information in the context of an event, story or dramatisation can be enormously helpful. Acting out an historical event, transforming a phonic rule into a little story, visiting the fire station and so on, are not simply devices to improve motivation; they also embrace the power of episodic memory to help children learn and remember. I recently came across a very effective way of remembering chemical equations which involved changing them into stories, devised in preparation for GCSE examinations. The process of photosynthesis, for example, became a moving love story between Mr Carbon and Miss Hydrogen, who met and were forever joined together. Such was their love that they constantly gave off little sounds of joy: 'O! O!' (Oxygen!) they would coo.

Semantic memory

Semantic memory is the latest evolving and uniquely human aspect of long-term memory because it depends upon our skill at symbolic representation, most significantly exemplified in our development and use of language. This is the part of our memories where we remember, rather than particular episodes or events, those thoughts, ideas, general rules, principles, concepts and so on which we infer from our particular experiences. Much more than either of the other long-term memory systems, semantic memory is subject to constant restructuring as we organise and re-organise our internal models of the world. As we gain more experience, we re-categorise items, we make new connections, and we invent, build and develop new hierarchies and webs of meaning.

In this system, it emerges that what determines how well remembered an item of information will be, and how easily it will be recalled, is dependent upon how well embedded, connected and elaborated it is within our semantic structures. The neoroscientific evidence suggests that this has two elements: the strength of connections and the extent of connections.

The Strength of Connections

As long ago as 1949, the psychologist D.O. Hebb postulated that learning consisted of forming connections between neurones in the cerebral cortex. These connections form when a pattern of neurones 'fire' together; the more often they fire together, the stronger the connection becomes. This essential model has been subsequently confirmed by neuroscientific research. The strengthening of connections does indeed occur through repetitious firing via the now well-established electrochemical mechanism of long-term potentiation (LTP).

This goes a long way to explaining the golden rule of learning, which is 'little and often'. If you want to learn anything, 10 minutes a day is much more effective than an hour a week because the former will oblige the learner to re-input the information on many more separate occasions, thus strengthening the neuronal connections. This probably also goes some way to explaining the evidence that once children have been introduced to some new information or ideas, in order to achieve long-term transfer, pedagogical practices which immediately require children to rehearse their new knowledge are highly effective. Children who are asked to learn some information and are then immediately tested on their recall of it, retain the information long term far more effectively than those who are not tested.

The Extent of Connections

As well as strengthening existing connections, learning also consists of constantly making new ones. When we are able to connect new information or ideas to ones we have already established, then we experience the new information as

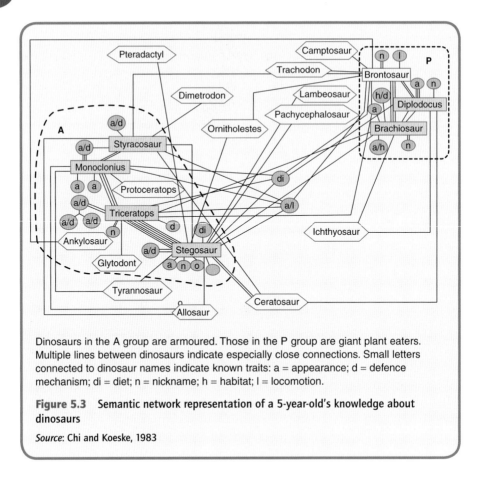

Dinosaurs in the A group are armoured. Those in the P group are giant plant eaters. Multiple lines between dinosaurs indicate especially close connections. Small letters connected to dinosaur names indicate known traits: a = appearance; d = defence mechanism; di = diet; n = nickname; h = habitat; l = locomotion.

Figure 5.3 Semantic network representation of a 5-year-old's knowledge about dinosaurs

Source: Chi and Koeske, 1983

having meaning or making sense. The more connections we can make, the more sense we can make of the new information, and the more likely we are to remember it. In order to demonstrate how this works, try to remember each of these 14-letter words. Look at them for 5 seconds, then cover them up and try to write them down.

    Constantinople   Gwrzcwydactlmp   χονοταντινοπλξ

Of course, you will have found the first one relatively easy, the second one difficult and the third one (unless you read Greek) completely impossible. This is clearly related to the extent to which you can connect these new pieces of information to your existing knowledge. The first is bristling with connections to things you already know, at several levels (meaning, phonic sounds, letters), whereas it is increasingly difficult to make any connections to the other two.

A delightful example of this crucial relationship between knowledge, meaning and memory was provided by Chi and Koeske (1983), who carried out a study of a 5-year-old budding dinosaur expert. This particular boy owned nine books about dinosaurs and could name 40 types. Figure 5.3 is a semantic network representation of his knowledge about dinosaurs that they constructed by asking him on six separate occasions to recall the names of dinosaurs he knew, and by seeing which clues he found most helpful in identifying dinosaurs. The dinosaurs were grouped by noting which ones he tended to remember together and which ones shared properties of which he was aware. As they hypothesised, on subsequent recall tests, the boy was most adept at remembering dinosaurs which had many links with other dinosaurs; the ones he tended to forget were the ones with fewest links.

Craik and Lockhart (1972) developed a model of memory which emphasises its close relationships with knowledge, meaning and understanding. This was known as the 'levels of processing' model within which they argued that the more 'deeply' new information is processed, the more likely it will be remembered. By 'deeply', they meant connected to existing knowledge and semantic networks. For example, they demonstrated that if we are given a list of words and asked to say if they are printed in capital letters or rhyme with 'lemon' (which require only superficial processing of the appearance or sound of the words), we are less likely to remember them than if we have to say, for example, whether they are animals or objects you would find in the kitchen (requiring deep processing of the words' meanings).

A number of very important implications for effective teaching flow from these insights into the processes within semantic memory. To begin with, it becomes very clear why it is so vital to help children connect new information or ideas to what they already know. We know that children are not nearly as efficient in searching their existing knowledge for connections to help them as adults; we need to construct strategies to help and encourage children to do this. When introducing something new, it is always helpful to remind children, or, even better, through careful questioning, oblige them to remind themselves, of what they already know that is related.

Second, when new information or ideas are being presented to children, it makes quite a remarkable difference if they are required to do something with it, rather than just passively receive it. In this regard, Howe (1999), for example, has written very persuasively about the importance of mental activity. If children are asked to re-express the idea in a variety of media (talking, writing, drawing, modelling, etc.), or asked to use the new information creatively, or use it to solve a problem, all of these processes will oblige them to make extensive connections, to re-organise their semantic networks and so on. In the process, the new learning will become securely embedded. This is, of course, as we discussed in the previous chapter, one of the important elements of what children spontaneously do when they engage in certain types of play.

SUMMARY

In this chapter, we have reviewed evidence accumulated by psychologists and neuroscientists which has helped us understand a good deal about the structure and development of human memory and the ways in which children learn and make sense of their world. Some very clear indications emerge as to what early years educators working with young children can do in order to help them remember and understand more effectively, as follows:

- gain their attention by making activities purposeful and personally relevant
- adopt a multi-sensory approach to activities
- place new tasks in familiar contexts
- encourage and foster children's self-monitoring of whether they have remembered something
- use explicit discussion and modelling to encourage children to try a wide range of memory strategies, when they have something to remember
- link new information to actions
- set new information in the context of an event, story or dramatisation
- require children to rehearse their new knowledge
- help children connect new information or ideas to what they already know
- make new ideas or information more memorable by requiring children to mentally process them, re-expressing them through talk, writing, drawing, modelling, play contexts, and so on.

These notions sound, in many ways, obvious and straightforward. They have very profound implications, however, for the planning and structuring of early years teaching. Applied imaginatively by skilled practitioners, what evidence we have suggests that they are capable of transforming children's developing abilities to remember, learn and make sense of the constant barrage of new ideas, information and skills with which they are confronted in and out of educational contexts.

QUESTIONS FOR DISCUSSION

- Why are some children much better at remembering than others?
- What can we do to make activities more memorable for those children who have difficulty with remembering?
- What types of activities or events do children find most memorable?
- As an adult, what do I do when I realise I am struggling to remember something?

ACTIVITIES

A. Memory strategies

Children can sometimes use strategies when they are suggested by a real situation, but cannot deliberately use them in isolation. For this procedure, you need to set up a situation in which there is a genuine need to remember – for example, a dinner party in the home corner and a shop on the opposite side of the room; or taking a message to another teacher; or asking the children to remind you about something later which is important to them. For comparison, you need to give the children something to remember which is equivalent but which they just have 'to remember' for no particular purpose, except you are going to ask them what they can remember later.

You need to make careful observations of the children's responses to these situations, particularly noting any signs of a strategy being used to help them remember the information, such as rushing before they forget, rehearsing, making connections or elaborations on what they have to remember. You should note down what they say at each stage, and record how much they could remember, and their apparent awareness of whether they had forgotten anything. Talk to the children afterwards about how they performed in their remembering tasks.

B. Metamemory

Children's knowledge about their own memory abilities, about memory strategies and about the ease or difficulty of different memory tasks, do appear to develop. In order to investigate this, you need a tray of 20 objects, some familiar and some unfamiliar to the children, and which are sortable into three to five categories. You then interview individual children and carefully record their responses, under these three headings:

1. Own abilities: show the child the tray of 20 objects, arranged randomly on the tray and covered over by a cloth, and ask them to estimate how many objects they will be able to remember if you let them look for 30 seconds. While they are looking you could note down any strategies they use. Record how many they are actually able to remember.
2. Strategies: ask the children what they could do to help themselves remember such a collection of objects.
3. Memory tasks: ask them how you could have made the 20 objects task easier; record any ideas the child has; if they do not offer much, make some suggestions (eg: arranging them differently, having fewer objects, giving them a longer time, choosing more familiar objects) and see how they respond.

References

Atkinson, R.C. and Shiffrin, R.M. (1968) 'Human memory: a proposed system and its control processes', in K.W. Spence and J.T. Spence (eds) *The Psychology of Learning and Motivation, Vol. 2*. London: Academic Press.
Baddeley, A.D. (1986) *Working Memory*. Oxford: Oxford University Press.
Baddeley, A.D. (2006) 'Working memory: an overview', in S.J. Pickering (ed.) *Working Memory and Education*. London: Academic Press.
Baddeley, A.D. and Hitch, G. (1974) 'Working memory', in G.H. Bower (ed.) *The Psychology of Learning and Motivation, Vol. 8*. London: Academic Press.
Bauer, P.J. (2002) 'Early memory development', in U. Goswami (ed.) *Blackwell Handbook of Childhood Cognitive Development*. Oxford: Blackwell.

Bruner, J.S. (1974) 'The growth of representational processes in childhood', in *Beyond the Information Given*. London: George Allen & Unwin.

Chi, M.T.H. (1978) 'Knowledge structures and memory development', in R.S. Siegler, (ed.) *Children's Thinking: What Develops?* Hillsdale, NJ: Lawrence Erlbaum.

Chi, M.T.H. and Koeske, R.D. (1983) 'Network representation of a child's dinosaur knowledge', *Developmental Psychology*, 19, 29–39.

Conway, M.A., Gardiner, J.M., Perfect, T.J., Anderson, S.J. and Cohen, G.M. (1997) 'Changes in memory awareness during learning: the acquisition of knowledge by psychology undergraduates', *Journal of Experimental Psychology*, 126 (General), 393–413.

Craik, F.I.M. and Lockhart, R.S. (1972) 'Levels of processing: a framework for memory research', *Journal of Verbal Learning and Verbal Behaviour*, 11, 671–84.

Dempster, F.N. (1981) 'Memory span: sources of individual and developmental differences', *Psychological Bulletin*, 89, 63–100.

Flavell, J.H., Beach, D.R. and Chinsky, J.M. (1966) 'Spontaneous verbal rehearsal in a memory task as a function of age', *Child Development*, 37, 283–99.

Hagen, J.W. and Hale, G.A. (1973) 'The development of attention in children', in A.D. Pick (ed.) *Minnesota Symposium on Child Psychology, Vol. 7*. Minneapolis, MN: University of Minnesota Press.

Hebb, D.O. (1949) *The Organisation of Behaviour*. New York: Wiley.

Howe, M.J.A. (1999) A *Teacher's Guide to the Psychology of Learning*, 2nd edn. Oxford: Blackwell.

Istomina, Z.M. (1975) 'The development of voluntary memory in pre-school-age children', *Soviet Psychology*, 13, 5–64.

Miller, G.A. (1956) 'The magical number seven, plus or minus two: some limits on our capacity for processing information', *Psychological Review*, 63, 81–97.

Nisbet, J. and Shucksmith, J. (1986) *Learning Strategies*. London: Routledge & Kegan Paul.

Ornstein, P.A., Grammer, J.K. and Coffman, J.L. (2010) 'Teachers' "mnemonic style" and the development of skilled memory', in H.S. Waters and W. Schneider (eds) *Metacognition, Strategy Use and Instruction*. New York: Guilford Press.

Tulving, E. (1985) 'How many memory systems are there?', *American Psychologist*, 40, 385–98.

Wellman, H.M. (1977) 'Tip of the tongue and feeling of knowing experiences: a developmental study of memory-mentoring', *Child Development*, 48, 13–21.

Chapter 6

Learning and Language

Key Questions

- What are the main theories of learning?
- In what ways is human learning different to that of other species, particularly other primates?
- Do adults think and learn differently from children?
- How do children develop as learners?
- Why are some children better learners than others?
- How does language help us to be better learners?
- How can we organise educational settings to support children's learning?

Early Behaviourist Theories of Learning

When I undertook my undergraduate degree in the late 1960s, I took a one-year course in learning theory. This represented an extremely thorough introduction to what psychologists at that point in time knew about learning and consisted almost entirely of experiments on rats, pigeons and the like learning to find their way through a maze or which lever to press to obtain a reward of food. This work was located within a school of psychology which is now referred to as behaviourism and was founded on the then very sensible proposition that, as we could not then directly observe and measure what was happening in people's brains or minds, if we wished to be scientific in our investigations of human psychology, we should confine ourselves to observing and measuring behaviour. This school of psychology was, to a degree, a reaction against earlier forays into understanding the workings of the human mind through the process of introspection, as practised by such early thinkers as William James (brother of the author Henry James).

In order to carry out truly scientific, rigorously controlled experiments, however, learning had to be reduced to very simple elements, removed from any kind of social context, and carried out on animals who could be confined, slightly underfed so that they were motivated by hunger, and treated in other ways which might not be considered as entirely acceptable or ethical with young children (even in the early part of the 20th century!). Perhaps the most well-known examples of this work are the Russian psychologist Ivan Pavlov's experiments with dogs, and the American B.F. Skinner's work with rats and pigeons. Pavlov showed that dogs could learn to associate a ringing bell with food, and eventzually would salivate at the sound of the bell alone. Skinner demonstrated that rats, pigeons, etc. could learn to press a lever to obtain food, and, given a choice of levers between which they could discriminate (such as by shape), they could learn to press the correct lever. He went on to show that what he termed a 'variable schedule of reinforcement' (when a correct lever press resulted in food randomly on some trials, but not all) was a far more powerful motivator to maintain a learnt behaviour than a fixed or regular schedule (when food was provided every time the lever was pressed, or every third time, for example). The parallel here with human gambling behaviour is quite striking. Imagine if fruit machines consistently just gave you back half of what you had put in every third go. The financial consequences would be the same, but not nearly so many people would travel to Las Vegas for the experience! Also, perhaps importantly for education, Skinner's work showed quite conclusively that providing a reward for correct behaviour was a far more efficient stimulus to learning than was punishing the animal when it made a mistake. Using his principles, he demonstrated that pigeons can count up to 7 and that they could be trained to roller-skate (two major scientific advances), but they are also the basis upon which dogs for the blind are trained, which underpin highly successful behaviour management techniques with children with severe conduct disorders, and sound principles used by many skilled early years teachers to help children learn how to behave in the social world of the school classroom. If we praise children when they are kind to one another, when they share their toys and so on, the classroom will become a far more harmonious place to be than if we concentrate on criticising and punishing behavioural lapses. According to one recent American study, involving 400 4–6-year-olds, who received stickers or verbal praise as rewards, it is even possible for young children to learn to like vegetables through these means (Cooke et al., 2011). I know – amazing, but true!

At the heart of behaviourism, then, there are a number of important insights that have been verified by later research. For example, as we shall see, the notion of learning as forming associations has been supported and extended in much more recent neuroscientific research (through which we can now directly observe the workings of the human brain). Nevertheless, despite these successes, it is clear that the behaviourists' model of human learning is quite inadequate. Indeed, this was gradually becoming clear in the 1960s when I was undertaking my own undergraduate education. In the introduction to his excellent book on children's learning, David Wood (1998) recounts this period when many young psychologists, trained in behaviourist methods, gradually became aware of the limitations of the approach. An important book (Hilgard, 1964), published at that time, represented a turning point in psychology's investigation of learning. In one chapter, for example, as Wood reports, a young psychologist called Pribram reported his experiences of experiments with monkeys which had caused him to doubt one of the major precepts of behaviourist theories of learning, that it relied upon external reinforcement (i.e. receiving food for a correct behaviour). One monkey, for example, quickly learnt to pull the correct lever, but then subverted the experiment by not eating peanuts it received on 'reinforced' trials, then feeding itself a peanut when the trial was not 'reinforced'. Eventually, when it had received more peanuts than it could eat, with its cheeks, hands and feet stuffed with them, it continued to pull the lever and, finally, to throw them out of the cage at the experimenter. Pribram concluded that the monkey's behaviour and learning could not be accounted for by the schedule of external reinforcement embodied in the experiment, but by the monkey's own 'intrinsic' interest in the task itself. He also, among a number of the contributors to the book, commented favourably on the new theories of children's learning being developed by the Swiss psychologist, Jean Piaget.

Piaget and the Constructivist Model of Learning

The fundamental problem with the behaviourist approach was that it characterised learning as an essentially passive process, consisting of forming simple associations between events, and being dependent upon external rewards or reinforcements. What was becoming increasingly clear in the 1960s, however, was that such a model could account quite well for the behaviour of relatively simple animals, such as rats or pigeons, but it could not account for learning in primates and was an entirely inadequate explanation of the richness, diversity and sheer creativity of human learning. As a consequence, when Piaget's work was translated and made available to the English-speaking scientific world, for example through the publication of John Flavell's (1963) book, *The Developmental Psychology of Jean Piaget*, it was greeted with enthusiastic acclaim. While much of the detail of Piaget's theory has now been discounted (as we discuss below), he is nevertheless rightly celebrated as the originator of a number of key insights into the nature of human learning.

Methodologically, he is celebrated for his demonstration that much can be learnt about children's learning and development by very careful naturalistic observation of children going about their everyday lives (much of his work was based on observations of his own children). As regards our understanding of the processes of learning, he is celebrated as the father of 'constructivism', which is the idea that children's learning is an active process through which they attempt to develop their skills and construct their own understandings of the world.

The kind of model of human learning which developed from this view is illustrated in Figure 6.1. Here, every aspect of the interaction between the learner and the environment is seen as active and dynamic. Rather than passively receiving information to be learnt, the learner actively perceives and selects the information they are seeking. The information is not simply stored, it is sifted, categorised and re-organised, patterns are detected and rules, 'schema' or concepts constructed. Similarly, the consequent actions or behaviour of the learner are not simply a 'response' to a 'stimulus' or a reward, as the behaviourists would have it, but are consequent upon hypotheses and predictions generated about the way the world works, and strategies and plans developed to act effectively upon it.

The example is often quoted of the way in which children learn language. According to a behaviourist view, this is a laborious process whereby every word and utterance the child learns is initially by imitating an adult and learnt as a consequence of reinforcement by external reward (such as adult smiling). However, it is clear that the rate at which children learn to understand and use language is far too rapid for this kind of explanation and, in any case, they typically produce a constant stream of completely novel utterances (in my family, we even have words and whole phrases which we now all use, but which were originally invented by the children). In English, many of these novel words and phrases that children produce, furthermore, are clearly the consequence of mis-applying patterns and rules which they have constructed for themselves. For example, you will hear young children say that yesterday they 'goed to the shops and buyed something'. They will not have heard an adult say this; nor has any adult taught them that you create the past tense by adding on 'ed'. This is a pattern or regularity that they have detected from the huge variety of their experience of spoken English.

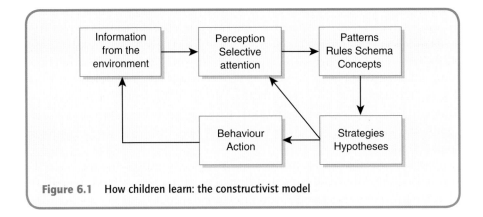

Figure 6.1 How children learn: the constructivist model

The Cognitive Revolution

Piaget was born in Neuchatel, Switzerland in 1896 and worked prodigiously until his death in 1980. His body of work was immense (around 50 books and 500 academic papers) and he is largely credited with having brought about what is termed the 'cognitive revolution' in psychological investigations of learning. The 'black box' psychology of the behaviourists (where the brain was seen as impenetrable and unobservable) was replaced by increasingly inventive and innovative methodologies and techniques which enabled psychologists in the latter part of the 20th century to explore much more directly the cognitive processes in the developing brain of the young child.

As it turned out, much of this work has directly contradicted Piaget's own theories about children's development, to the point where today the specifics of his theories are largely dismissed. As we shall see, the main criticisms of his work arise from his failure to take into account the social nature of learning, and the important role of social interaction and language in children's developing abilities as learners. As a consequence, in many of his studies, he set children tasks where they performed poorly because of the linguistic demands of the task, and misleading social clues, rather than because of an underlying failure of understanding. This led him, it is now believed, to significantly underestimate the capabilities of young children.

One of the earliest researchers to expose these limitations in Piaget's work was a Scottish psychologist, Margaret Donaldson. In her classic text, *Children's Minds* (Donaldson, 1978), she reports a number of studies where slight variations in the way in which Piaget's tasks were presented to children showed them to be much more capable than he had suggested. For example, Piaget's famous number conservation task consisted of showing the child two equal rows of buttons (as shown in Figure 6.2, Part 1) and asking the child whether there are more white buttons or black buttons, or whether they are the same. One of the rows was then transformed by the experimenter (as shown in Figure 6.2, Part 2) and the question was repeated. Piaget found that many young children could correctly recognise that the first two rows contained the same number, but said there were more white buttons in the second condition. He concluded that these young children were overwhelmed by their perceptions and that they lacked the logical understanding of the conservation of number.

When this task was repeated, however, by a colleague of Margaret Donaldson's, the transformation of one of the rows of buttons was effected by a 'naughty teddy' glove puppet. In these circumstances, many more young children were able to say that the two rows still contained the same number.

Donaldson concludes that the introduction of the naughty teddy changes the meaning for the child of the second question. This question is made sense of by the children in relation to the social situation and their own previous experience. When the adult transforms the pattern and repeats the question, this means to

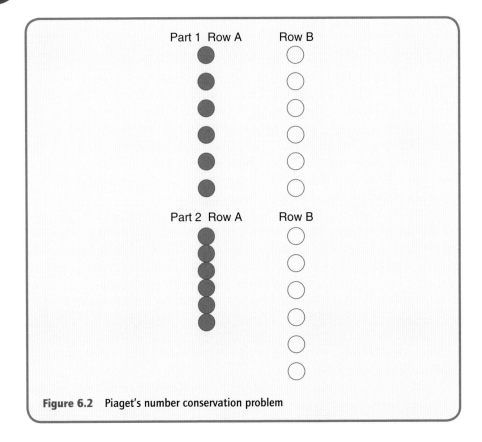

Figure 6.2   Piaget's number conservation problem

some children that their first answer was wrong and the adult is helping them to see the correct answer. In the amended version, the second question is a cue to check that the naughty teddy hasn't lost or added any buttons during his mischief.

What is more, lest we think that such reliance on the social context of a task is a sign of immaturity in children's thinking, it is now clearly established that human adults' thinking is equally reliant on these kinds of social cues, and that we all find abstract reasoning problems much more difficult than ones placed in a socially meaningful context or scenario. Wason and Johnson-Laird (1972), for example, posed the following 'four-card' problems (see Figure 6.3 for a slightly updated version). In the numbers and letters version (a), we are told that each card has a number on one side and a letter on the other. Your task is to name those cards, and only those cards, which need to be turned over in order to determine whether the rule (set out below the cards) is true or false. In the 'people with drinks' version (b) (my own cunning invention but with less skilful drawings), we are asked to pretend that we are working in a bar which serves beer and tea (stay with me) and where, to help preserve the law about under-age drinking, everyone is given a sticker on their back showing their age. Your job is to make sure that no one is breaking the law, i.e. you have to say which of the four people,

If a card has vowel on one side, then it has an even number on the other side.

If you are drinking beer, you must be at least 18 years of age.

Figure 6.3   The four-card problem

Source: Wason and Johnson-Laird, 1972

and only which people, you would need to turn round to make sure that customers are obeying the law set out below the drawings. Write down your answers before you read on and find out if you have a typical human adult brain!

The correct answer to (a) is the vowel (E) and the odd number (7) – not the even number (4), which is a popular choice, but wrong since it would not contradict the rule if there were a vowel or consonant on the other side. Similarly, the correct answer to (b) is the person drinking beer and the person who is only 16. Most adults (even those brainy enough to be reading this book!) find the more abstract version (a) difficult and often make mistakes. The more socially contextualised version (b) is nearly always found to be much easier, although logically it is an identical problem. Ironically, this dependence upon the social contexts of tasks both makes sense in relation to the social origins of human evolution, as we have discussed in earlier chapters, but is also a logical consequence of Piaget's own theoretical position, that we construct our own understandings from experience.

This kind of work, by Donaldson, Wason and Johnson-Laird and many others, is important for developmental psychologists, as we try to unravel the complexities of the development of the human brain, but it also has some highly significant implications for those of us involved in the education of young children. Young children do not passively receive the information we provide for them. They are engaged continually in a process of active interpretation and transformation of new experiences and the information derived from them. If we want to help young children make sense of their educational experiences, we must ensure that we place new tasks in contexts with which they are familiar and which carry meaning for them.

Beyond this, through a range of newly emerging technologies, such as habituation (to which we referred in the Play chapter), eye-tracking, computer modelling and neuroscientific techniques, cognitive psychologists over the last 30 years or so, have uncovered an impressive range of processes by which the human brain learns. They have also established that many of these processes are there and fully functioning at birth, or mature very quickly during the first 4 to 5 years of life, as the brain increases in size fourfold (largely as a consequence of a rapid increase in the number of synaptic connections between neurons in the cerebral cortex). Goswami (2008) has provided an extensive review of the many experiments which have shown the very early emergence of this range of basic learning processes.

One such process which seems to be there from birth is referred to as statistical or inductive learning. This is the process by which we identify patterns and regularities in the stream of experience, and is fundamental to a very large proportion of human learning. It might be seen as a much more sophisticated and active form of association learning, of the kind explored by the behaviourists, and it clearly underpins the ways in which the human visual system learns, how young children learn language with such rapidity and ease, how they form concepts and detect categories from their experience, and how they seem so ready and able to understand causal relationships between events. Using habituation techniques, researchers have shown that, for example, babies as young as 2 months old can learn complex sequence patterns in a series of shapes they are shown, and will subsequently show a preference for 'novel' patterns which are made up of the same shapes but do not contain the same sequences (Kirkham et al., 2002). The patterns used, to a great extent, mirrored those found, for example, in language, involving 'transitional probabilities' of one shape following another, rather than just fixed sequences. Astonishingly, the 2-month-olds were just as proficient at this as babies 6 months older.

As we discussed in the previous chapter, neuroscientific work on memory has established that semantic information is stored in the cerebral cortex through a process whereby neurons establish increasingly stronger connections between themselves. So, the kinds of patterns (or rules, 'schema', or 'concepts' – see Figure 6.1) learnt through these processes of statistical or inductive learning appear to be physically held in networks of interconnected neurons. Quite a body of recent research, referred to as 'connectionist modelling', has attempted, with some success, to model neural networks that might be responsible for particular aspects of learning. So, for example, Plunkett (2000) has reviewed some of the key ideas and conclusions from this type of work and has reported, for example, very successful attempts to model young children's typical vocabulary growth, using a computer simulation.

Figure 6.4 shows a graph of a typical vocabulary learning trajectory, in which, after a period of relatively slow but steady growth over several months, there is a sudden spurt at around 22 months. As those of us who work with young children know, this kind of 'discontinuity' is very common in many areas of young children's learning. Plunkett and colleagues managed to construct a surprisingly simple neural network which learnt vocabulary (i.e. could reliably name a series of objects correctly) and produced a pattern of learning remarkably similar to that typically seen in vocabulary growth. What this seems to indicate is that the long plateaux and then sudden spurts so typical of young children's learning are a structural consequence of the ways in which the neuronal networks in the human brain learn.

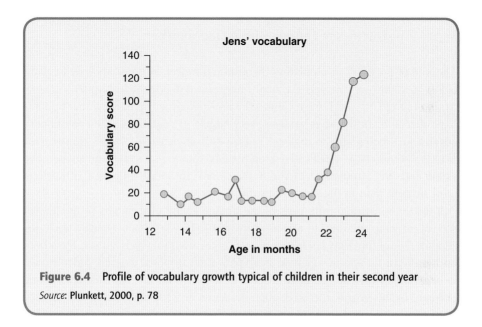

Figure 6.4   Profile of vocabulary growth typical of children in their second year

Source: Plunkett, 2000, p. 78

Closely related to these statistical or inductive processes, whereby patterns are actively constructed from experience, are processes of learning by analogy. This is an entirely active form of learning, perhaps not quite unique to humans, but infinitely more developed than in any other species, whereby a pattern identified and learnt in one context is used to make sense of a new experience or new information related to a separate context. This ability, sometimes referred to as the 'transfer' of learning, or 'generalisation', is of enormous significance in explaining human adaptability to new situations, and human capability in regard to novel problem solving. The vast changes in human civilisation and technology, since our ancestors lived as nomadic hunter-gatherers, would not have been possible without the ability to learn by analogy. Contrary to Piaget's conclusion that analogy is a complex form of reasoning which does not develop until later in development, Goswami (1992) was one of the first to demonstrate that it is, indeed, present in young children. She showed that children as young as 4 years old could reason analogically, provided that they understood the basic relationships involved. So, for example, a child of this age shown a pair of pictures of a bird and a nest could pick out a picture of a kennel to go with a dog. Chen et al. (1997), however, went further and managed to demonstrate basic analogical learning in children as young as 10 and 13 months. Their task involved learning a sequence of moves in order to retrieve an attractive doll (remove a barrier, pull a sheet with a string lying on it, then pull the string to move the doll). At these ages, the children required an adult to model the basic series of moves, but once learnt, they could then apply them (the 13-month-olds rather more flexibly than the 10-month-olds) to other similar tasks.

Social Constructivism: Learning from One Another

The role of the adult in modelling the required moves in the study by Chen and colleagues, however, reveals the final important component in human learning. At the start of Chapter 3, we reviewed the now widely accepted view that humans have developed in the ways we have, very largely in response to the evolutionary advantage of being able to organise ourselves in increasingly larger groups. This placed a premium, as we discussed, on the development of social and cooperative skills, and this attunement of the human brain to social influence is nowhere more evident than in the realm of learning.

It is also, intriguingly, the basis of the unique ability of members of the human species (of some relevance to readers of this book, I hope!) to deliberately teach one another. One of the many fascinating aspects of the ways in which humans learn from one another, is the way in which we are so powerfully disposed to teach, and to engage in behaviours which are perfectly adapted to support learning, particularly in young children. In this regard, the production by adults of what has usually been termed 'motherese' is an excellent example in relation to children's learning of language, and it points up very clearly the advantage of adults mediating children's experience for them (of which more later) in order to assist in the process of identifying patterns and regularities in their experience. When adults speak to babies and infants, they typically enunciate more clearly, use a more 'sing-song' voice exaggerating the intonations and stresses in speech, use a more limited vocabulary and shorter, simpler sentences, referring to the here-and-now, and respond to the child's productions in ways which would be odd, or even rude, if they appeared in adult-to-adult conversations (for example, repeating what the child says, or expanding a child's utterances into complete sentences). We all do this, without anyone teaching us, and it clearly helps young children to develop their receptive and expressive language.

Applying this approach to other areas of children's learning is often a characteristic of someone who is described as a 'natural' teacher, and, as we shall see, there are individual differences in adults' sensitivity and responsiveness to young children which have a clear impact upon children's learning. Within developmental psychology, the social interaction processes which relate to children's learning have been examined mainly in regard to learning by imitation (which relies, in the teaching context, on adult modelling) and learning through social interaction (which relies on the use of language).

Learning by imitation

We now know, chiefly through the work of American developmental psychologists Andrew Meltzoff (briefly mentioned in Chapter 3) and Keith Moore (Meltzoff and Moore, 1999), that young children are astonishingly adept at learning through imitation, from a very early age. In a paper published in the late 1970s, Meltzoff and Moore reported video data showing clear evidence of babies of 12 to 21 days old imitating both facial and manual gestures (see Figure 6.5). As is always the case with evolved behaviours, humans not only show the ability to imitate one another from a very early age, but brain mechanisms have also evolved to reward ourselves for doing it. We derive enormous pleasure, as children, and as adults, from imitating one another and being imitated. Imitative behaviour is often associated with playfulness and laughter; it is no accident, for example, that it is the basis of much adult comedy and satire, as well as many children's games.

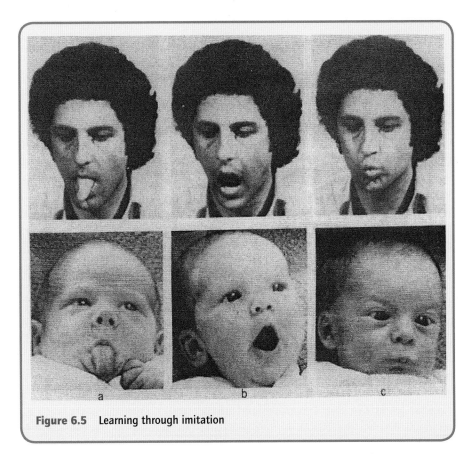

a   b   c

Figure 6.5   Learning through imitation

But it is worth considering what a phenomenal achievement even simple physical imitation represents. For a very young baby to be able to observe an adult performing an action, and then to be able to recognise which parts of its own body are equivalent, and, within its own immature motor cortex, to organise itself to perform the same action, shows a level of cortical organisation from birth which was not recognised until very recently indeed. Intriguingly, there is now some fairly strong evidence to suggest that this is achieved by what has been termed the 'mirror neuron' system (Rizzolatti and Craighero, 2004). What seems to be the case is that these same neurons fire, both when we observe another person performing a particular action, and when we perform it ourselves. This system seems to be fundamental to imitative behaviours, but also, in relation to issues discussed in Chapter 3, to understanding others' minds and intentions, and to empathetic responses to others' emotional states.

Within the context of learning, however, the ability to imitate the actions of another is clearly of enormous benefit in relation to learning a physical skill (for example, in learning a craft or in sports coaching – I am currently developing a golf swing of astonishing beauty by watching Tiger Woods!). In humans, furthermore, it is enormously enhanced as a tool for learning by the ability for imitation which is not only immediate (i.e. carried out while the to-be-copied behaviour is still perceptually available) but also deferred (i.e. performed on a subsequent occasion). Deferred imitation appears to be unique to humans as, of course, it crucially depends upon our ability to mentally represent objects and events in memory. This ability again appears to be present from a surprisingly early age, and to develop rapidly in very young children. Piaget observed deferred imitation in his own young children as long ago as the 1960s (Piaget, 1962), but only when they reached 16–24 months. In more recent work, Meltzoff (1988) identified deferred imitation in children as young as 9 months old. At this age, he demonstrated that they could reproduce novel actions they had observed up to 24 hours later (when presented with the same toy), but later work has shown that by 18 months this is up to two weeks, and by 24 months children are capable of showing deferred imitation after delays of 2 to 4 months. These are enormously valuable findings which inform our understanding of the development of young children's representational abilities, and their ability to hold mental representations in long-term memory.

Learning through social interaction

Modelling and imitation are, of course, a simple form of social interaction, and one can commonly observe adults and babies deriving enormous pleasure from pulling faces and blowing raspberries at one another. The astonishingly early predisposition and ability in babies to interact with others, and the powerful predisposition in adults to interact with babies and to read meaning into their actions and vocalisations, has been beautifully documented in the work of Colwyn Trevarthen (see Trevarthen and Aitken, 2001). Over many years, based on detailed video analysis of mother and child interactions, he has persuasively argued that they are best characterised as 'proto-conversations' within which the early establishment of children's abilities to derive meaning through interaction, or 'inter-subjectivity', is established. For example, he argues that:

> The interactions are calm, enjoyable and dependent upon sustained mutual attention and rhythmic synchrony of short 'utterances' which include, beside vocalisations, touching and showing the face and hands, all these expressions being performed with regulated reciprocity and turn-taking. Newborn and adult spontaneously display a mutually satisfying inter-subjectivity. (Trevarthen and Aitken, 2001, p. 6)

The establishment of 'mutual' attention is clearly a key element in these early communicative episodes. This develops within the first two years of life, it appears, as the growing child develops the ability for 'shared' attention, i.e. the ability to jointly attend, with an adult, to an external object or event. This most obviously emerges initially through the use and understanding of the pointing gesture. By 10–12 months, infants typically point to objects of interest which are out of reach and, shortly afterwards, they acquire the ability to locate objects pointed out to them by others (like most other primates, children under the age of 9 months respond to a pointing gesture by looking at your finger – try it!). During the second year of life, children then gradually acquire the ability to establish joint attention by following an adult's gaze. Once again, the predisposition of adults to support this development, by closely monitoring the infant's gaze, looking where they are looking, and using this focus of attention as the basis for further interaction (for example, by naming the object, commenting upon it, or fetching it for the child) has been clearly documented (Butterworth and Grover, 1988).

Extensive studies of these early adult–child interactions, however, have shown that, while there is a general disposition to support these early communicative developments, there are considerable variations in the sensitivity and style of communication between adults, and that these variations are clearly related to individual differences in children's learning, particularly in relation to language development. To begin with, a number of studies have shown that there are considerable differences in the amount of time 1-and 2-year-old children spend in joint attention episodes with their parents or caregivers (including joint play, conversation, book reading) and that this variation is related to the rate of language development of the child. Further, within joint attention episodes, significant differences exist in the sensitivity, or responsiveness, of parents or caregivers to their children, and this also impacts upon language development. Some adults appear to be much more aware of the child's pointing gestures or gaze as indicators of their focus of attention, and, having established the child's focus, some adults tend to use this as a basis for further interaction, including talk, while others tend to attempt to switch the child's attention to their own focus of interest. Not surprisingly, the former 'attention-following' strategy, building on the child's current interest and attention, has been found to support language development much more effectively than the 'attention-shifting' approach (for a review of this work, and research on language development generally, see Schaffer, 2004).

These findings are clearly of considerable interest to early childhood educators. Supporting early language development is clearly important in itself, if we wish to help children to become articulate adults, but it is even more important given its established relation to the ease with which children make the transition into literacy, and the now compelling evidence that, in the phrase popularised by Jerome Bruner, language is a 'tool of thought'. As regards the first issue, particularly given the current obsession in the UK with teaching young children 'phonics' divorced from meaning, I can do no better than recommend a recent excellent review by Catherine Snow, who has been foremost in research in this area for many years (Snow, 2006). As she notes, the two established predictors of literacy ability in early childhood are vocabulary size and phonological awareness. However, as she also notes, and as I would wish to argue, given what we know about children's learning more generally, direct instruction of vocabulary or phonology may not be the most productive approach. As we have seen, young children's learning is enormously enhanced by new information being placed in contexts which are of current interest to them and are, therefore, in a real sense, meaningful. Of course, it is perfectly possible to introduce the phonology of the written form of the language to young children in ways they find interesting. Given this, Snow cites rather strong evidence (from a meta-analysis of a considerable body of research) that about 20 hours of attention to phonological awareness is sufficient for almost all children (Ehri et al., 2001), and that supporting children to write, with their own attempts at spelling, supports phonological awareness as effectively as explicit curricula.

Language and learning: the contribution of Vygotsky

It is to the issue of the role of language in learning that I wish to turn in the final section of this chapter. The ideas of the Russian psychologist, Lev Vygotsky, to whom we have referred in Chapter 4 in relation to children learning through play, have been enormously influential in this area. While Piaget had argued that language development was a product of children's general ability to learn, and their increasing abilities for mental representation, Vygotsky argued the exact reverse. Happily, for those of us engaged in the education of young children, the evidence now overwhelmingly supports the Vygotskian view.

Piaget had emphasised the importance of the child interacting with the physical environment, and his followers in the educational sphere argued that the role of the teacher should be that of an observer and a facilitator. The general view of this approach was that attempting to directly teach or instruct young children was a mistake. It was claimed that whenever teachers attempted to teach children something, they simply deprived the children of the opportunity to discover it for themselves. This view was partly a reaction against the simplistic 'behaviourist' model that children only learnt what they were taught, and were rewarded for learning (as we have outlined in the first part of this chapter). This view, however, can be seen to have thrown the baby out with the bath water.

More recent research, inspired by the work of Vygotsky, has shown that there is a much more central role for the adult, and, indeed, for other children, in the processes of learning. This role is not as an instructor delivering knowledge, however, but rather as a 'scaffolder' (a metaphor suggested by Jerome Bruner and colleagues – Wood et al., 1976) supporting, encouraging and extending the child's own active construction of meaning and understanding. Based on observational studies of mothers and young children in experimental contexts, this group of researchers developed a characterisation of scaffolding which supports and develops many of the ideas emerging from other studies of early interactions, as we have reviewed above. So, they determined that a good scaffolder engages the interest of the child, simplifies the task if necessary, highlights critical features of the task, models key processes or procedures and, perhaps most importantly, sensitively monitors the child's success with the task and withdraws support when the child can proceed independently. The parallels with the work on adults supporting children's language learning are evident.

The central idea in Vygotsky's model of children's learning is that all learning begins in the social context, which supports children in the processes whereby they construct their own understandings. Thus, he argued that all learning exists first at the 'inter-mental' level (i.e. within the experience of joint attention and inter-subjectivity) in the form of spoken language, and then at the 'intra-mental' level (i.e. within the child's mind, in the form of internal language, or thought). This has been termed the 'social constructivist' approach to learning. Within this model, a further key insight is that of the 'zone of proximal development' (ZPD), as illustrated in Figure 6.6. Faced with any particular task or problem, Vygotsky argued, children (or any other learners for that matter) can operate at one level on their own, described as their 'level of actual

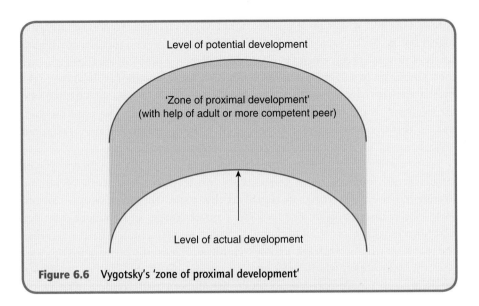

Figure 6.6   Vygotsky's 'zone of proximal development'

development', but at a higher level when supported or 'scaffolded' by an adult or more experienced peer, described as their 'level of potential development'. The ZPD is that area of learning between these two levels of performance or understanding, within which the child is really challenged, but which they can achieve with appropriate support.

Vygotsky and his followers have further argued that children learn most effectively through social interaction, when they are involved in jointly constructing new understandings, within their ZPD. Intriguingly, this view has been supported by a range of research, including that related to young children's production of what has been termed 'private speech', when they self-commentate on their own activities (to which we referred also in Chapter 4). Vygotsky's view was that this represents a crucial bridging mechanism between external 'social speech', produced in the context of social interaction with an adult or peer, and fully formed 'inner speech', which we all use as adults to help us to structure and keep track of our thoughts. It appears predominantly in young children up to the age of 7 or 8 years, and then gradually fades, as the capability for 'inner speech' is established, but is still commonly observed in older children and adults when they are dealing with a particularly challenging problem.

If Vygotsky's model is correct, it would be predicted that private speech would support young children's thinking and would be produced by young children at the highest rate when they are required to deal with a problem that is in their ZPD. It would also be predicted that the production of private speech would enhance children's problem-solving abilities. Extensive research into the phenomenon of private speech has fully supported both of these predictions (Fernyhough and Fradley, 2005, Winsler and Naglieri, 2003). The production of private speech by any individual child graphed against the level of difficulty of a task produces an inverted U shaped curve, or what might be termed a 'Goldilocks' pattern. That is, tasks which are too easy or too difficult lead to relatively low levels of private speech, but tasks which are at just the right level of challenge lead to significantly higher levels. At the same time, between children, those who produce the higher levels of private speech when faced with a challenging problem are those who are most successful in solving it. I have known early years practitioners who have told me that they have tended to discourage young children from talking to themselves; the evidence would suggest that we should be doing exactly the opposite and, indeed, that the incidence of 'private speech' is an excellent indicator of children being involved in tasks which they find appropriately challenging.

This view has been further supported by evidence of the significant role of language development more generally within learning. The work of Jerome Bruner has been influential in regard to this issue (see, for example, Wood, 1998, for a discussion of Bruner's ideas on language and thought). Bruner described language as a 'tool of thought', and demonstrated in a range of studies the ways in which language enables children to develop their thinking and perform tasks which would otherwise be impossible. In his famous '9 Glasses Problem' (see Figure 6.7), for example, he showed that children who could

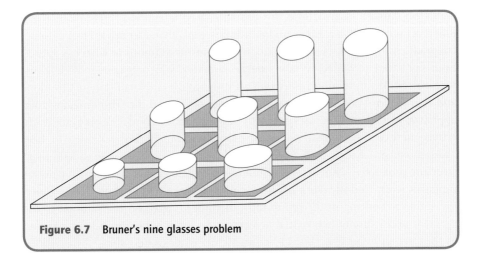

Figure 6.7 Bruner's nine glasses problem

describe the patterns in a 3 x 3 matrix of glasses (which were taller or shorter one way and thinner or fatter the other) were also able to transform the matrix (i.e. arrange the glasses in a mirror-image pattern). Children without the relevant language to call on, however, were only able to reproduce the pattern exactly as they had seen it.

It is now widely recognised that providing children with a relevant vocabulary and requiring them to formulate their ideas in discussion is a vital element in helping children to develop flexibility in thinking and construct their own understandings about the world. As long ago as the 1980s, Tizard and Hughes (1984), in a classic study of 4-year-old girls attending pre-school in the mornings, and spending time with their mothers at home in the afternoons, presented evidence of these young children engaging in intellectual search through conversations with their mothers. The kinds of meaningful dialogues they shared with their mothers, unfortunately, were sadly lacking in their pre-school experience. Sylva and colleagues (Sylva et al., 2004), more recently, in a large longitudinal study of factors leading to effective early years educational provision, have shown that high quality pre-school experience can significantly impact upon a range of intellectual and personal gains, even over-riding the effects of social disadvantage, for example, and that a key element in high quality provision appeared to be the occurrence of episodes of 'sustained shared thinking' between adults and children.

This kind of evidence has led to the recognition that a certain style of interaction between adults and children, along the lines emerging from the research we have reviewed in this chapter, and between pairs or small groups of children, can be enormously beneficial to learning. A range of recent and current classroom-based research has supported this view and has begun to identify in more detail the specific elements of a successful 'dialogic' pedagogy appropriate for children in the early years of education (Mercer and Littleton, 2007). Neil Mercer and colleagues

(Littleton, Mercer et al., 2005), for example, have identified three qualitatively different kinds of talk in young children's discussions, characterised as Disputational (unproductive disagreement), Cumulative (uncritical additions to what has already been said) and Exploratory talk (involving active joint engagment with ideas, where assertions and counter assertions are supported by explanations, justifications and alternative hypotheses). They have further developed the 'Thinking Together' approach, which incorporates tasks to support children's developing ability to engage in exploratory talk in group discussions, including activities to help children construct their own agreed 'rules for talk' and to use these to help them structure productive joint activities. Interestingly, one key element which emerges from this work, and the work of Howe and colleagues (Howe et al., 2007) is that the children working in the group must attempt to agree on the solution to the problem under discussion. Actual agreement does not appear to be as important as the attempt to achieve this. Littleton, Mercer et al. (2005) showed that young children could make significant strides in their ability to argue their case and provide explanations for their views, and that there were measurable gains in both the quality of their language and their non-verbal reasoning skills.

In a current piece of research which I have been conducting with Neil Mercer, with 5- and 6-year-old children in Year 1 classrooms, we have shown that this kind of approach can also encourage young children's self-regulation, measured both by their teachers' observational assessments (of which more in Chapter 7) and by their ability to reflect upon and talk about their performance on particular tasks. A recent American study (Vallotton and Ayoub, 2011) of 120 toddlers in New England has established a similarly exciting relationship between vocabulary size (which they distinguished from general 'talkativeness') at ages 14, 24 and 36 months and observed self-regulatory behaviour (such as the ability to maintain attention on tasks, and to adapt to changes in tasks and procedures). What emerges from this whole area of research is that a primary and fundamental goal of any early years educator must be to extend the language knowledge and skills of the young children in their care, as the evidence is now overwhelming concerning the significance of this area of development to learning in its broadest sense. Silence, in the modern early years classroom or setting, is anything but golden.

SUMMARY

We have seen that, as developmental psychologists have explored learning, we have become increasingly aware of the range and sheer power of the ways in which humans learn, right from the moment they are born. Piaget can be credited with having first established the dynamic, active model of young children's learning which is widely accepted today. But the particulars of his model of development, which characterised children as limited by logical deficiencies in their reasoning powers, have been largely dismissed. As Margaret Donaldson (1978) and others have demonstrated, adults make the same kinds of logical errors as children, and have difficulties with the same kinds of reasoning problems, particularly when they are divorced from meaningful contexts (as Philip Wason's four-card problem so brilliantly illustrates). In contemporary developmental psychology, children's learning is seen as being limited much more simply by their lack of experience and of accumulated knowledge. This makes it more difficult for them to see what is relevant in any new situation, and to see what is the best way to proceed. When this is made clear by the context in which a task is presented, however, children's potential for learning is phenomenal and often way beyond what was appreciated even quite recently. For those readers interested in what we know currently about the capabilities of very young children, I would enthusiastically recommend Tiffany Field's *The Amazing Infant* (2007), or either of Alison Gopnik's excellent books in this area (Gopnik, 2009; Gopnik et al., 1999). If you want to see what a 3-year-old can do, given the opportunity and the love and support, go to this YouTube clip (I promise you, it is amazing!): www2.choralnet.org/268945.html

The current view of the child as learner is one which recognises their considerable appetite and aptitude for learning, and the very active nature of learning processes, including statistical or inductive learning, learning by analogy, learning by imitation through social interaction with adults and more experienced peers, and learning through the formation of mental representations using language.

We have also seen how views about the role of the adult in supporting children's learning have veered from the early behaviourist view (beloved of our politicians) that children will only learn what they are taught, to the opposite Piagetian view that children must learn by themselves and adults getting involved will only interfere. The current view, supported, as we have seen, by a considerable and diverse body of evidence, is rather more measured and nuanced. The role of the adult (and peers) in supporting children's learning is established, but is seen not as that of an instructor, but rather as that of a facilitator and mediator, a more experienced tour guide taking children to all the important beauty spots in the world of learning, and pointing out the key cultural icons to which they should especially pay attention. As early years educators, in undertaking this role, the research evidence from developmental psychology we have reviewed in this chapter provides us with a number of clear principles to guide our practice, as follows:

- Children do respond to external rewards, such as stickers and verbal praise, but these represent a limited view of children's learning, and can encourage a passive, dependent style of learning in young children, so are perhaps best reserved as a means of dealing with anti-social and supporting prosocial behaviour in the early years; verbal praise for prosocial behaviours is far more effective than criticism of undesirable behaviour.
- Children are powerfully dynamic and active learners, who are highly motivated to learn about and make sense of their world; this is best supported by providing them with activities placed in contexts which are meaningful to them and relate to their current interests and enthusiasms.

(Continued)

(Continued)

- From a very early age, perhaps even a few weeks old, many of the processes through which the human brain learns are already in place; this includes learning by identifying patterns and regularities in the flow of experience and learning by imitating the actions of adults and older peers.
- During the first year or two of life, the learning of common patterns and regularities supports the ability to understand new experiences by analogy, and deferred imitation becomes an important part of the young child's learning repertoire.
- Much of this learning is supported by social interaction with adults and peers; from the first few weeks of life infants engage in 'proto-conversations' with adults, and their early endeavours to make meaning of their experiences are strongly supported during episodes of joint attention with adults during the first few years of life; these episodes are much more productive when the adult responds to and develops the child's focus of attention, rather than trying to re-direct the child's attention to a predetermined focus.
- In particular, these episodes of joint attention are instrumental in supporting children's language development; through a 'motherese' style of speech, adults help children to discern regularities in language, to develop their phonological awareness and their listening and speaking abilities, and to extend their vocabulary; in turn, these abilities support young children's early engagement with written language.
- Language is also a powerful 'tool of thought'; children's developing abilities to use language as a tool for learning is most powerfully supported by the experience of engaging in meaningful dialogues with adults and peers; in these contexts, adults can most purposefully 'scaffold' children's engagement with tasks or activities which would otherwise be slightly beyond their capabilities; the social speech used in these dialogic contexts is later used by young children, in the form of 'private speech', to enable them to undertake the same or similar tasks independently.
- Young children can learn to engage in productive 'exploratory' talk with peers, unsupported by an adult, provided they are given the opportunity to reflect upon and agree 'rules for talk', and are provided with collaborative problem-solving tasks which are appropriately structured to encourage genuine discussion and expression of views supported by arguments and explanations.

QUESTIONS FOR DISCUSSION

- Should we praise children when they have completed a task successfully, or should we ask them to explain how they did it?
- How can we help children to understand the important points or ideas in any new activity or area of knowledge we are introducing?

- How can we ensure that we spend time each day engaging productively in extended discussions with the young children in our care?
- Is teaching young children 'phonics' an important component in supporting their language and literacy development?

ACTIVITIES

A. Talking to children

Tape record some conversations with individual children, each lasting at least 2–3 minutes. In some of these conversations, decide beforehand on something you wish to 'teach' the child, and make a point of asking the child a number of questions to check their understanding. In other conversations, allow the child to determine the topic of discussion, listen to what they say and try to help them say more about their experiences and ideas, and share with the child some of your own experiences or thoughts.

These conversations could be stimulated by sharing a storybook, or by engaging in a joint activity (such as playing together with dough or a construction toy). Afterwards, listen to the conversations and answer the following questions:

- Who did most of the talking?
- Was it a genuine conversation, in which we both enjoyed sharing ideas and experiences, or was it just a question and answer session, with the child being fairly monosyllabic?
- Did I help develop the child's vocabulary?
- Did I help develop the child's ability to explain a narrative or justify an opinion?
- Do I feel I now know the child better, and appreciate his/her interests and concerns better than I did before?
- Do I see how I could do it better next time?

B. Private speech

Observe (or, ideally video-record) individual children engaged in construction or imaginative play. Note examples of their speech which do not seem to be directed at anyone else but are just 'private speech' to themselves. See if you can find examples of the following:

- *Planning*: talking about what they intend to do, or need to do next, or what they are trying to achieve
- *Monitoring*: talking about what is happening or what they are doing at that moment
- *Instructing*: talking to themselves to direct their current activity
- *Evaluating*: talking about how well they have carried out an activity, or how good they are at this kind of thing generally
- *Playing with sounds and words*: singing, humming, making sounds or exclamations to accompany the activity
- Inaudible mumbling.

Do you notice some children engaging in more of this private speech than others? Do you notice children producing more private speech when they are engaged in some kinds of activities than others?

C. Supporting 'exploratory talk'

In developing young children's abilities to organise productive discussions amongst themselves, it is best to start with some preparatory activities. Of course, children cannot usefully discuss activities of which they have no experience, so it is a good idea to set up a number of opportunities for them to try to have a discussion in small groups first. These generally work best if the activities are open-ended, require the children to make a decision, and cannot be solved in a straightforward manner. For example, try one of these:

- sorting out into groups a random collection of objects which do not fall into obvious categories; you could either decide on the number of groups to be formed or leave this open
- putting a set of five works of art in order from most to least favourite, as agreed by the group
- casting a puppet show: choosing from a selection of puppets which ones should play which characters in a well-known story.

After each of these sessions, discuss with the children how well it went and what problems they had in coming to an agreement. Ask them if they did all genuinely agree or if one member of the group made all the decisions. After a few trials, you can start to pick out with the children what you need to do to have a good discussion. Perhaps you could model good discussion and bad discussion with some puppets? Then set up further discussion activities for the children to decide their own 'rules for talk' for the class (see Dawes and Sams, 2004, for some proven ways of doing this, the associated issues and lots of excellent ideas for ways to extend this work further).

References

Butterworth, G.E. and Grover, L. (1988) 'The origins of referential communication in human infancy', in L. Weiskrantz (ed.) *Thought without Language*. Oxford: Oxford University Press.

Chen, Z., Sanchez, R.P. and Campbell, R.T. (1997) 'From beyond to within their grasp: the rudiments of analogical problem-solving in 10- and 13-month-olds', *Developmental Psychology*, 33, 790–801.

Cooke, L., Chambers, L., Anez, E., Croker, H., Boniface, D., Yeomans, M. and Wardle, J. (2011) 'Eating for pleasure or profit: the effect of incentives on children's enjoyment of vegetables', *Psychological Science*. Available at: http://dx.doi.org/10.1177/0956797610394662

Dawes, L. and Sams, C. (2004) *Talk Box: Speaking and Listening Activities for Learning at Key Stage 1*. London: David Fulton.

Donaldson, M. (1978) *Children's Minds*. London: Fontana.

Ehri, L.C., Nunes, S.R., Willows, D.M., Valeska Schuster, B., Yaghoub-Zadeh, Z. and Shanahan, T. (2001) 'Phonemic awareness instruction helps children learn to read: evidence from the National Reading Panel's meta-analysis', *Reading Research Quarterly*, 36, 250–87.

Fernyhough, C. and Fradley, E. (2005) 'Private speech on an executive task: relations with task difficulty and task performance', *Cognitive Development*, 20, 103–20.

Field, T. (2007) *The Amazing Infant*. Oxford: Blackwell.

Flavell, J.H. (1963) *The Developmental Psychology of Jean Piaget*. Princeton, NJ: Van Nostrand.

Gopnik, A. (2009) *The Philosophical Baby*. London: The Bodley Head.

Gopnik, A., Meltzoff, A.N. and Kuhl, P.K. (1999) *How Babies Think*. London: Weidenfeld & Nicolson.

Goswami, U. (1992) *Analogical Reasoning in Children*. London: Lawrence Erlbaum.

Goswami, U. (2008) *Cognitive Development: The Learning Brain*. Hove, East Sussex: Psychology Press.

Hilgard, E.R. (ed.) (1964) *Theories of Learning and Instruction*. Chicago, IL: University of Chicago Press.

Howe, C.J., and Tolmie, A., Thurston, A., Topping, K., Christie, D., Livingston, K., Jessiman, E. and Donaldson, C. (2007) 'Group work in elementary science: towards organizational principles for supporting pupil learning', *Learning and Instruction,*17, 549–63.

Kirkham, N.Z., Slemmer, J.A. and Johnson, S.P. (2002) 'Visual statistical learning in infancy: evidence for a domain general learning mechanism', *Cognition*, 83, B35–42.

Littleton, K., Mercer, N., Dawes, L. Wegerif, R., Rowe, D. and Sams, C. (2005) 'Talking and thinking together at Key Stage 1', *Early Years*, 25, 167–82.

Meltzoff, A.N. (1988) 'Infant imitation and memory: nine-month olds in immediate and deferred tests', *Child Development*, 59, 217–25.

Meltzoff, A.N. and Moore, M.K. (1999) 'Imitation of facial and manual gestures by human neonates' and 'Resolving the debate about early imitation', in A. Slater and D. Muir (eds) *The Blackwell Reader in Developmental Psychology*. Oxford: Blackwell.

Mercer, N. and Littleton, K. (2007) *Dialogue and the Development of Children's Thinking: A Sociocultural Approach*. London: Routledge.

Piaget, J. (1962) *Play, Dreams and Imitation in Childhood*. New York: W.W. Norton & Co.

Plunkett, K. (2000) 'Development in a connectionist framework: rethinking the nature–nurture debate', in K. Lee (ed.) *Childhood Cognitive Development: The Essential Readings*. Oxford: Blackwell.

Rizzolatti, G. and Craighero, L. (2004) 'The mirror neuron system', *Annual Review of Neuroscience*, 27, 169–92.

Schaffer, H.R. (2004) 'Using language', in *Introducing Child Psychology*. Oxford: Blackwell.

Snow, C.E. (2006) 'What counts as literacy in early childhood?', in K. McCartney and D. Phillips (eds) *Blackwell Handbook of Early Childhood Development*. Oxford: Blackwell.

Sylva, K., Melhuish, E. C., Sammons, P., Siraj-Blatchford, I. and Taggart, B. (2004) *The Effective Provision of Pre-School Education (EPPE) Project: Technical Paper 12 – The Final Report: Effective Pre-School Education*. London: DfES/Institute of Education, University of London.

Tizard, B. and Hughes, M. (1984) *Young Children Learning*, London: Fontana.

Trevarthen, C. and Aitken, K.J. (2001) 'Infant intersubjectivity: research, theory and clinical applications', *Journal of Child Psychology and Psychiatry*, 42, 3–48.

Vallotton, C. and Ayoub, C. (2011) 'Use your words: the role of language in the development of toddlers' self-regulation', *Early Childhood Research Quarterly*, 26, 169–81.

Wason, P.C. and Johnson-Laird, P.N. (1972) *Psychology of Reasoning: Structure and Content*. London: Batsford.

Winsler, A. and Naglieri, J.A. (2003) 'Overt and covert verbal problem-solving strategies: developmental trends in use, awareness, and relations with task performance in children aged 5 to 17', *Child Development*, 74, 659–78.

Wood, D.J. (1998) *How Children Think and Learn*, 2nd edn. Oxford: Blackwell.

Wood, D.J., Bruner, J.S. and Ross, G. (1976) 'The role of tutoring in problem-solving', *Journal of Child Psychology and Psychiatry*, 17, 89–100.

Chapter 7

Self-regulation

Key Questions

- What is meant by independent learning, 'self-regulation' and metacognition?
- Why is it important for children to develop the ability to be self-regulatory learners?
- What is the relationship between emotional, social, cognitive and motivational aspects of self-regulation?
- How can we support and encourage the development of metacognitive and self-regulatory skills in young children?
- How can we assess children's self-regulatory abilities?

What is Meant by Self-regulation and Why is it Important?

In the first chapter of this book, I set out my intention to argue that, based on the evidence emerging from developmental psychology, particularly in the last 30 years or so, it is now clear that young children are far more capable than was previously thought. In particular, I argued that children are far more capable of taking responsibility for their own learning, or of becoming 'self-regulating' learners, than was thought even only two or three decades ago. I also pointed out, however, that while there has been a good deal of enthusiasm recently for developing young children as independent or self-regulating learners within governments internationally, and among the early years educational community, there has been considerable confusion about what exactly this means, at both a theoretical and practical level. In particular, I am very keen to distinguish self-regulation from what might be termed 'compliance' or some of the narrower conceptions of 'school readiness'. Self-regulation refers to fundamental aspects of emotional, social, cognitive and motivational development and is not at all the same thing as being ready to do what you are told, or being ready and willing to sit still and be quiet. However, it is the basis for the development of a wide range of skills and dispositions which are very strongly associated with children becoming successful learners, and socially adept and successful adults. It is therefore vitally important that, as early years practitioners, we clearly understand the nature of self-regulation and how it might be most effectively supported and fostered in young children.

I hope that the contents of the intervening chapters in this book have helped to clarify the way in which self-regulation is understood, at least within developmental psychology. I also hope it is also clear why it is regarded as so important. We have seen that developing increasing self-awareness, leading to increasing control of their own mental processing and performance, is relevant and fundamental across the whole range of children's development. This is just as true of becoming aware of one's own emotional experiences, and one's own social abilities, as it is with regard to one's own cognitive processes underlying the abilities which help us to learn, think, reason and remember. Powering all this, in turn, is young children's intrinsic and active desire to make sense of their world, to be in active control of their own experiences, and to make relationships with other children and adults. We have also seen, I hope, that children's essentially playful nature provides perfectly adapted contexts within which all these developments can thrive.

In this final chapter, I want to pull all this together and to review some of the research and theory specifically related to developing self-regulation, so that its essential elements are further clarified. I also wish to attempt to draw out more clearly the very significant implications for practice in supporting the learning and development of young children in the early years of their education.

There are three very clear traditions within developmental psychology which have contributed to current understandings regarding self-regulation. These come from those post-Piagetian psychologists who contributed to the cognitive revolution we reviewed in Chapter 6, from the Soviet school of psychology of which Vygotsky was the leading theorist, and from 'social' psychologists interested in understanding human motivations.

Among the first group, American psychologist John Flavell is generally recognised as the first to specifically identify and recognise the significance of what he termed 'metamemory' and then 'metacognition'. In a classic series of experiments in the 1960s and early 1970s, to which we referred in Chapter 5, he explored young children's failure to use memory strategies in relation to particular memory tasks even when they knew the strategies, and had successfully used them on a previous occasion (Flavell et al., 1966). Flavell's momentous insight was to realise that children as young as 5 years old might be able to carry out a verbal rehearsal strategy, when asked to remember a list of objects for 20 seconds, but might not realise that this would be an appropriate thing to do. And, as we saw, when he went on to teach them to do so, the 5-year-olds showed themselves to be perfectly capable of verbally rehearsing, and of performing at the same level as older children. However, when they were subsequently presented with a very similar task, about half of the 5-year-olds again failed to rehearse and produced a poor memory performance. Flavell coined the term 'production deficiency' to account for this pattern of behaviour among the 5-year-olds, arguing that what had still to develop was not their ability to perform verbal rehearsal but their ability to know when and why this strategy should be adopted. This he subsequently termed a deficiency in the youngest children's 'metamemory', i.e. their knowledge about their own memory processes and how to use them, combined with their awareness of whether what they were doing was working, or if they needed to adopt a different approach or strategy.

As we further reviewed, however, evidence from subsequent studies has shown that this apparent deficiency in the young children's metacognitive awareness was, at least in part, a consequence of the experimental situation. This is reminiscent of some of the work critical of Piaget's early studies. So, for example, in the study to which we referred in Chapter 5, carried out in the mid-1970s by the Russian psychologist, Z.M. Istomina (1975), children as young as 5 years were shown to be perfectly capable of showing awareness of their own memory processes, and using appropriate strategies, when the context of the task was meaningful to them. Here is Istomina's record of the performance of a 5-year-old girl called Alochka on a memory task involving shopping for the doll's lunch:

Alochka (five years, two months) was busily engaged in preparing lunch, and several times reminded the experimenter that she needed salt.

When it was her turn to go to the store, she asked, with a busy expression on her face:

'Z. M., what should I buy? Salt?'

The experimenter explained to her that this was not all and named four more items that were needed. Alochka listened attentively, nodding her head. She took the basket, the permission slip and money and went off, but soon came back.

'Z. M., I have to buy salt, milk, and what else?' she asked. 'I forgot.'

The experimenter repeated the items. This time Alochka repeated each word after the experimenter in a whisper and, after saying confidently, 'Now I know what I had forgotten,' went off.

In the store, she went up to the manager and, with a serious expression, correctly named four items, with slight pauses between each.

'There is something else, but I forgot,' she said. (Istomina, 1975, pp. 25–6)

We can clearly see here evidence of emerging metacognitive awareness in Alochka. Throughout, she is aware of what she has remembered and what she has forgotten. To begin with, she tries the simple strategy of 'nodding her head' for each item on the list, but quickly realises this hasn't worked. So, the second time, she uses a different strategy, 'repeat(ing) each word after the experimenter in a whisper', and this is much more successful. This is an excellent example of metacognitive processing in action, involving monitoring the current state of one's knowledge or memory, or how well what you are doing is working, in order to achieve your goal, and making adjustments to the cognitive strategies you are using in order to improve your performance. This is precisely what we do as adults when, for example, we are reading a text. As we read, we constantly monitor whether we are understanding the ideas being developed, or the latest twist in the plot. If we notice that we are not understanding, we then adopt one from our repertoire of reading strategies to remedy the situation. So, we might read the last passage again, with greater concentration; we might flick back through the book to an earlier, related section; we might look forward to see where the argument is going; we might look up a word in the dictionary, and so on. We might even decide we are losing concentration because it is late or we are tired, and have a coffee or take a break, or go to sleep and try again in the morning. All of this depends upon our well-developed metacognitve abilities.

The now accepted model of this metacognitive processing is that developed by Nelson and Narens (1990), a version of which is presented in Figure 7.1. Essentially, they suggest that, as we undertake mental tasks, we are operating on at least two levels simultaneously (even men!). At the 'object' level, we are actually carrying out the task, but at the same time, at the 'meta' level, we are holding in mind the goal of the task and accessing stored information about the task or similar tasks (by analogy) from long-term memory derived from previous experience. We are also, at the meta level, comparing our progress with the desired goal, and adjusting what we are doing at the object level, if required. This is achieved by information flowing from the object level to the meta level (monitoring) continuously updating our representation of our progress on the task at the meta level, and information flowing in the opposite direction (control) continuously adjusting the cognitive strategies used. Through development, the accumulated metacognitive knowledge derived from previous experience leads to increasingly efficient performance of this feedback loop, and ensures that our cognitive activity on a well-known task is increasingly smoothly coordinated, automatic and efficient. We may be conscious of some of this processing (perhaps mostly so when we are a novice in relation to any particular task) but much of this happens completely without our conscious awareness.

When a task is relatively new or novel, however, the necessary metacognitive activity requires considerable effort and may well overload the capacity of the young child's working memory (as we also discussed in Chapter 5). This view is supported by a number of other, more recent studies, providing evidence of metacognitive activity by young children in tasks which are more age-appropriate. Deloache et al. (1985), for example, demonstrated the development of error-correction

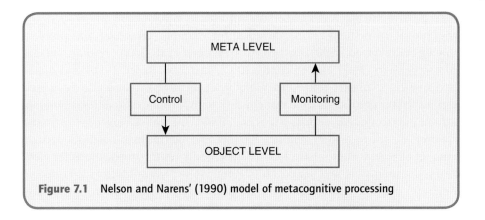

Figure 7.1   Nelson and Narens' (1990) model of metacognitive processing

strategies in young children's manipulative play from as early as 18 months. Blöte et al. (1999) studied the organisational strategies of 4-year-olds using a new kind of 'same–different' task which involved sets of toys and was structured to minimise memory demands (the children had to decide whether two sets of seven toys were the same – containing an identical set – or not). They found that, with this task, the children's spontaneous behaviour was highly strategic and, although most children did not spontaneously use the most effective 'matching' strategy, they could be trained to do so and were able to transfer this strategy to new materials. They thus demonstrated that the 'production deficits' of young children revealed in the early studies of Flavell and colleagues may well be a consequence of problems with working memory load rather than metacognitive processes as such. In my own work, to which I return later in the chapter, we have also identified metacognitive and self-regulatory behaviours within playful activities in children as young as 3 years. Bronson (2000) has provided an excellent review of the now considerable body of research cataloguing the gradual emergence and development of self-regulatory abilities, across the cognitive, emotional, social and motivational domains in children from birth up to the end of primary school.

There can be no doubt, however, that children's metacognitive abilities, while present in emergent forms from very early in life, do develop considerably as they grow older and into maturity, and also that they vary considerably between children (and adults!). Both these points are of enormous educational significance. In a review of the extensive literature up to that point, Wang et al. (1990), for example, concluded that metacognition was the most powerful single predictor of learning. More recently, Veenman et al. (2004) have shown that metacognitive skilfulness makes a unique contribution to learning performance beyond that accounted for by traditionally-measured intelligence.

The significance of an individual's ability to monitor and regulate their own cognitions, and to develop increasingly sophisticated metacognitive knowledge about their own capabilities, about different tasks and cognitive strategies, has been demonstrated across a wide range of human development and areas of the educational curriculum.   This includes, for example, reasoning and problem solving (Whitebread, 1999), mathematics (de Corte et al., 2000), reading and text comprehension (Maki and McGuire, 2002), memory (Reder, 1996) and motor development (Sangster Jokic and Whitebread, in press). It has also been well established for quite some time that children with learning difficulties commonly exhibit metacognitive deficits (Sugden, 1989). As the emergence in young children of self-regulatory abilities has become increasingly acknowledged, a number of recent studies have focused specifically on the implications for early years education. Blair and Razza's (2007) study of 3–5-year-olds from low-income American families, for example, showed that aspects of self-regulation (particularly inhibitory control, of which more later) predicted progress in early maths and reading abilities approximately a year later.

Pedagogies Supporting Self-regulation: Vygotsky and Social Interaction

Happily, the origins of the marked individual differences observed in metacognitive and self-regulatory skills and dispositions are illuminated by the research from the other two research traditions to which we referred above. Work deriving from the theoretical ideas developed by Lev Vygotsky, and from 'social' psychologists interested in understanding human motivations, have combined to provide explanations of how the early difficulties with working memory capacity and the effort required to act metacognitively are overcome by a combination of adult support and the rewards arising from successful performance.

  Research based on Vygotsky's theoretical model of the development of self-regulation has also begun to show how metacognitive learning might occur and how it might be encouraged in educational contexts. For Vygotsky, the development of children's learning was a process of moving from other-regulation (or performing a task while supported by an adult or peer) to self-regulation (performing a task on one's own). As we discussed in Chapter 6, perhaps the most famous of Vygotsky's ideas is what he termed the 'zone of proximal development' (ZPD), which is the zone between what the child can do currently on her own and what the child can do given some support from an adult or more experienced peer. Vygotsky went on to suggest that it is when the children are operating in their ZPD that the most powerful and effective learning occurs. All learning for Vygotsky, therefore, starts socially. As we further reviewed in Chapter 6, a considerable body of research work in recent years has investigated the processes by which adults support children's learning. This research has largely endorsed Vygotsky's approach, and has also identified the elements which make some adults particularly effective in supporting and promoting children's learning in the ZPD. Adults encourage, instruct, ask questions, simplify the task, remind children of the goal, make suggestions, model to emphasise the key points, give feedback, and so on. These various forms of interaction combine so that the skilful adult provides what has been termed 'scaffolding', a temporary support structure which enables the child to successfully carry out any particular task, and so build their skills and understanding. Crucially, however, research has shown that a key characteristic of a good scaffolder is the ability to sensitively withdraw support as the child becomes able to carry out the task more independently, and to take over more of the regulatory role for themselves (for an excellent review of work in this area, see Schaffer, 2004).

Learning for Vygotsky can therefore be characterised as a process of internalisation, whereby the procedures for successful completion of a task are initially modelled and articulated by an adult or more experienced peer, with the child then gradually becoming able to talk themselves through the task using self-commentary or 'private speech'. Finally, the child can fully self-regulate using internal speech or abstract thought. This model would suggest that metacognitive and self-regulatory skills are learnt through social interaction, which, if true, is an extremely exciting prospect for early years educators. A now extensive literature, concerned with developing and evaluating educational interventions intended to promote metacognitive and self-regulatory abilities in young children, has confirmed Vygotsky's position and shown that they are indeed highly teachable.

Helpfully, Dignath et al. (2008) have recently completed an up-to-date meta-analysis of studies focusing specifically on self-regulation interventions with children of primary school age. Such interventions show consistently positive results. Typically, these interventions have involved making metacognitive and learning strategies explicit, and encouraging children to reflect upon and talk about their learning. Several pedagogical techniques of this kind have been investigated and developed. These include:

- 'cooperative groupwork' (Forman and Cazden, 1985): a range of techniques involving children in collaborative activities which oblige them to articulate their own understandings, evaluate their own performance and be reflective about their own learning
- 'reciprocal teaching' (Palincsar and Brown, 1984): a structured procedure which involves teachers modelling the teaching of a particular task to children who are then asked to teach the activity to their peers
- 'self-explanations' (Siegler, 2002): an instructional practice which requires children to give 'how' and 'why' explanations about, for example, scientific phenomena or the events in a story, and then asks children to give explanations of their own and an adult's reasoning (where the adult says what they think and then asks the child why they think the adult thinks that, or how they came to that answer or conclusion)
- 'self-assessment' (Black and Wiliam, 1998): a range of pedagogical ideas involving children's self-assessment of their own learning, including, for example, children making their own choices about the level of difficulty of tasks to be undertaken, and selecting their best work for reflective portfolios

- 'debriefing' (Leat and Lin, 2003): a range of techniques for reflecting upon an activity or piece of learning, including 'encouraging pupils to ask questions', 'making pupils explain themselves' and 'communicating the purpose of lessons'.

While many of these original studies were carried out with older children, in my own research I have worked with skilled early years practitioners to examine their viability with children as young as 3 years of age, and we have always found that they are adaptable to the younger age group, enthusiastically responded to by the children and highly effective in supporting children's self-regulatory development. In the Cambridgeshire Independent Learning project (C.Ind.Le; Whitebread et al., 2005, 2007), to which I have referred in earlier chapters, the 32 early years teachers involved, working with 3–5-year-olds, demonstrated the efficacy of a number of these pedagogical techniques, and were delighted with the evident impact upon their children's ability to talk about their own learning, and to develop confidence as learners within educational contexts. In a more recent study with Neil Mercer, as I reviewed in Chapter 6, Year 1 teachers working with 5–6-year-olds were equally delighted by the impact of supporting their children to learn to engage in productive collaborative problem solving and discussion.

One further issue arising from these various studies is worthy of emphasis. It has been consistently found to be crucially important that children are provided with the opportunity to reflect on the effectiveness of the strategies they have used. Young children, in particular, will often show that they are capable of using a strategy (just as they did in Flavell's original memory experiments), and that their performance improves when they do so. However, unless they attribute their improved performance specifically to the use of the strategy, they are unlikely to transfer its use to similar tasks. Fabricius and Hagen (1984), for example, taught an organisational strategy to 6- and 7-year-olds which improved their performance on a memory task. Following this improved performance, some of the children attributed this to the use of the strategy, but others failed to monitor the cause in the difference in their own performance and thought they had recalled more because they had looked longer, used their brains more or slowed down. Perhaps not surprisingly, while only 32% of the children in the latter group transferred the use of the strategy to a second recall task, 99% of those who explicitly recognised the impact of the organisational strategy they had been taught did so. In my own recent study with Neil Mercer in Year 1 classes, therefore, a discussion with the children of how well their group work had gone, and why it was more successful when they followed their 'rules for talk', were an essential component of the debrief part of the lesson.

Pedagogies Supporting Self-regulation: Emotional, Social and Motivational Elements

There is, however, a further important element in our understandings concerning children's developing self-regulation, and this relates to the contribution made in this area by 'social' psychologists interested in understanding human motivations.

This arises from the recent and important recognition in this area of research that metacognitive abilities have an impact on behaviour and performance, but that this also depends upon the degree of effort that the individual decides to exert in relation to any particular task. The individual's beliefs about the value of the task, their emotional response to it – i.e. feelings of difficulty, level of interest, personal relevance, etc. – and the reasons they attribute to previous success and failure on similar tasks, will all impact upon what Paul Pintrich (2000) and others have referred to as their 'goal-orientation' (i.e. what their personal goals are in doing the task) and thus their metacognitive performance. As any early years teacher will immediately recognise, however well planned an activity might be, if it does not capture the interest of the children, then their efforts will be focused in other directions, and they will not concentrate their efforts on the task sufficiently for it to be a worthwhile experience. The research concerned with 'attention-following' and 'attention-shifting' adult styles in episodes of joint attention, which we reviewed in Chapter 6, is clearly relevant here. This recognition of the importance of motivation has led Paris and Paris (2001) to refer to self-regulated learning as the 'fusion of skill and will'.

The relationships between cognitive and motivational aspects of self-regulation have become a strong element of recent research. Schunk and Zimmerman's (2008) edited collection helpfully contains reviews of much of the significant work in this area. This includes work related to 'self-efficacy' (children's belief that they can improve their abilities through effort, leading to a 'mastery' orientation rather than to 'learned helplessness'), to interest (leading to engagement and involvement) and to 'self-determination' (which suggests that the satisfaction of children's needs for feelings of competence, autonomy and 'relatedness' – or, positive social relationships – crucially impact on their ability to take command of their own motivations and regulation). While metacognitive theorists have increasingly recognised the significance of motivation, correspondingly those studying emotional development (as we reviewed in Chapter 2) have increasingly recognised the significance of metacogntive aspects of developing emotion regulation. This has culminated, for example, in the emergence of the model of emotional intelligence developed by Daniel Goleman (1995).

Understandings emerging from neuroscience have also supported a model which integrates emotional and cognitive aspects of self-regulation. The development of metacognitive, self-regulatory executive functions appears to be related to developments in the frontal lobes. Barkley (1997), for example, synthesised several models of frontal lobe functioning and proposed five executive functions which together comprise a comprehensive and integrated self-regulatory system. These five components, which clearly contain cognitive and affective elements, are as follows:

- inhibition, which allows automatic or ongoing processes to be stopped or interrupted
- working memory, which allows the recall of past events and planning for the future

- internalised speech, which allows for self-regulated, conscious functioning on current tasks
- motivational appraisal, which allows constraints to be placed on decision making by emotions and motivation
- 'reconstitution' or behavioural appraisal, which allows for the analysis and re-organisation of behaviour.

What is exciting here is that each of these components of frontal lobe functioning clearly relates to theoretical constructs identified within the developmental psychology literature. We have reviewed the work related to working memory in Chapter 5, and to internalised speech in Chapter 6. We will refer to inhibition towards the end of this chapter, when we look at the assessment of self-regulation. The notion of the appraisal of emotions, motivations and behaviour is a fundamental element in current models of development in these areas, which we partly addressed in Chapter 2 in relation to emotions, and to which we return when we consider approaches to motivation below. This concurrence of psychological and neuroscientific evidence gives us tremendous confidence in the validity of the self-regulation model.

A range of empirical studies has confirmed the theoretical interrelationships between metacognitive and emotionally and motivationally self-regulatory processes. Pintrich and De Groot (1990), for example, explored relationships between reported motivation, self-regulated learning and academic achievement in a large sample of seventh graders. Their findings indicated that positive self-efficacy beliefs and intrinsic task value were positively related to reported use of cognitive and metacognitive strategies and to persistence in the face of difficulty. In other words, students who believed they were capable and students who showed genuine interest in their school work were more likely than other students to deploy cognitive strategies and regulate the use of these strategies when performing tasks.

In another study, Pekrun et al. (2002) explored the role of emotions in self-regulated learning. Some of the relations reported in their study showed distinctive patterns for emotions such as enjoyment and hope versus emotions such as anxiety and boredom. Positive emotions were positively related to effort, interest, use of elaboration strategies and self-regulation and negatively related to irrelevant thinking. Negative emotions showed the opposite pattern, being negatively related to interest, effort, elaboration strategies and self-regulation and positively related to irrelevant thinking and external regulation.

Associated with this developing recognition of the significance of emotional and motivational elements, a number of studies have moved away from just examining the impact of the direct teaching of metacognitive skills and strategies to focusing on the social and emotional aspects of educational environments which might support the development of self-regulation. Two exemplary studies which illustrate this new emphasis in theory and research are Perry's (1998) observations of second and third grade classrooms during literacy activities and the work of Meyer and Turner (2002) on the scaffolding discourse of teachers in sixth grade maths lessons.

Perry (1998) observed second and third grade classrooms doing literacy activities over a period of 6 months and, through observations and interviews with the young students, she explored the impact of types of tasks, forms of assessment and authority structures on the students' regulation during writing tasks, and perceptions of support and control as well as beliefs, value judgements and expectations in relation to reading activities. Based on her observations, she identified two different types of classrooms: high and low self-regulated learning (SRL) classrooms.

High-SRL classrooms were characterised by challenging and open-ended writing activities; opportunities for children to control the level of challenge and opportunities for them to engage in self-assessment; autonomy support through strategy instruction, and encouragement of a mastery-oriented approach fostering positive feelings towards challenge and emphasising personal progress and mistakes as opportunities for learning. In contrast, in low-SRL classrooms children were more likely to be engaged in restricted types of activities with limited choices. Evaluation procedures were mainly controlled by the adult and were similar for all students emphasising performance and triggering social comparison. The observation of the performance of these students revealed that the students in the high-SRL classrooms were more able than the students in the low-SRL classrooms to engage in systematic and strategic approaches towards the tasks, operating in a flexible way and seeking assistance appropriately. The students' reports in semi-structured and retrospective interviews also indicated important differences. While the students in the high-SRL classrooms showed prevalence of a mastery-oriented approach which was evident even in students with low ability, the students in the low-SRL classrooms were more prone to avoid engagement in challenging tasks and to show motivational vulnerabilities (Perry et al., 2002).

Similar findings emerged from Meyer and Turner's (2002) exploration of the scaffolding discourse of sixth grade teachers in maths lessons. Three different categories of scaffolding were explored: (a) scaffolding understanding; (b) scaffolding of autonomy through strategy instruction and gradual transfer of responsibility, and (c) scaffolding of the classroom environment emphasising positive feelings, collaboration and mastery-orientation. In parallel, two categories of non-scaffolded instruction were identified: (a) teacher-controlled responses and (b) non-supportive responses. The findings from this research indicate that students who reported higher indicators of SRL participated in classrooms characterised by: (a) positive and supportive classroom climates; (b) a strong focus on understanding; (c) encouragement of autonomy by shifting responsibility from the teacher to the students; and (d) shared responsibility for learning.

The C.Ind.Le Project: Developing Self-regulation in the Foundation Stage

While these particular studies are clearly with slightly older children, within my own research in the C.Ind.Le project, as I outlined in the very first chapter, we identified key characteristics for a pedagogy of self-regulation in early years classrooms and settings under the general headings of emotional warmth and security, feelings of control, cognitive challenge and the articulation of (i.e. talking about) learning. I have reviewed this work and its implications for the organisation of early years classrooms in more detail elsewhere (see, for example, Whitebread et al., 2008), and conclude this chapter, and this book, in the Summary section below, with some thoughts and ideas which have emerged from observations in early years classrooms where children are clearly being supported to develop as self-regulated learners.

The major achievement of the project, however, was to show that children as young as 3 years of age do show clear evidence of emerging self-regulatory skills within educational contexts, and can be supported and encouraged to develop these further. We collected around 100 hours of video in 32 different Foundation Stage settings throughout Cambridgeshire (including those working in urban, rural, socially deprived and affluent, suburban areas). Within this data, we identified around 600 episodes which showed clear evidence of self-regulatory behaviour, evidenced by clearly observable verbal and non-verbal behaviours. Self-regulation behaviours were observed when children were playing alone, or in small groups, or involved in large group or whole-class discussions. They were observed in the presence and absence of adults, both indoors and outdoors, and across the range of the curriculum. Significantly, however, they were most commonly observed in contexts involving activities initiated by the children, and when the children were playing in small groups, either working together to solve a problem (such as completing a floor jigsaw, building with construction materials) or engaged in some kind of imaginative socio-dramatic role play. I have published elsewhere more detailed accounts of the evidence emerging from this project (Whitebread et al., 2005, 2007).

As part of the C.Ind.Le project, we also developed a 5-day training course which has been rolled out across Cambridgeshire Foundation Stage settings, and which has been remarkably successful, I think, principally because of the reception that the approaches we have developed have been given by the children. At the end of the course, participants are required to identify one aspect of their practice, or one area of their setting or classroom, which they would like to change and improve. But they are also required to consult the children at every stage of the process, including the planning, development and evaluation of the innovation. Participants are often, understandably, anxious about this project, but are unanimous afterwards in their enthusiastic appreciation of what they have learned, and how the children have benefited, from them daring to take this leap of faith. They often comment on a wide range of improvements to the children's commitment and involvement in their activities, to improvements in the social life of the classroom, and to their own understanding of how they can develop their pedagogy to support, rather than impede, the children's development as learners. It has been a real joy to have shared these revelations with these practitioners, and I hope some of that enjoyment of young children's energetic and unfettered enthusiasm for learning, given the opportunity to show their true capabilities, has come across in the pages of this book.

Assessment of Self-regulation in Young Children

In the earliest research concerned with metacognition and self-regulation, the focus was very largely on adults and older children, mostly due to the restrictions of limited methodologies. For example, self-report questionnaires have been widely used in this literature, together with 'think aloud' techniques, where the subject is asked to say out loud what they are thinking as they undertake the experimental task. Both of these methods are clearly unusable with young children. The advent of digital video and sophisticated video analysis software, however, has made it possible to analyse large volumes of observational data of the kind collected in the C.Ind.Le project, and this has stimulated an increasing interest in self-regulatory behaviours in young children. The observational analyses conducted within the C.Ind.Le project have enabled us to identify the characteristic behaviours which signal the healthy development of self-regulatory abilities among children in the 3–5 age range. This has been developed into the Children's Independent Learning Development (CHILD) observational instrument, which can be used within research contexts, but is also for use by class teachers. In later research, we have shown that this instrument has good validity, relating clearly to other more experimental measures of metacognitive abilities (Whitebread et al., 2009), and can be reliably used by early years practitioners to assess self-regulatory development in young children. We have also been told by many practitioners that it usefully complements the formal assessments arising from the EYFS profile and forms the basis for much more meaningful discussions with parents concerning their children's development. The list of the 22 statements included in the CHILD instrument, and exemplar events providing evidence of these abilities in young children, are reproduced in Figure 7.2. In the suggested activities at the end of this chapter, I have outlined how you might begin to use the CHILD instrument, if you would wish to do so, in ways which many early years practitioners have found to enhance their understanding of self-regulation in young children, and to help them develop their own practice to support these important aspects of development. I have also outlined some simple tasks which have been developed and widely used in research studies to assess young children's inhibitory control (i.e. their ability to stop themselves doing one thing and deliberately control their actions to do something else), which is now clearly established as a fundamental cognitive building block in children's development of their self-regulatory development. I wish you well in your endeavours in this area.

Statement	Exemplar Event	Description
EMOTIONAL ELEMENTS OF INDEPENDENT LEARNING		
Can speak about others' behaviour and consequences	Warning about paper clips	Three children are playing in the workshop area. A girl that appears to be leading the game is explaining to the rest of the group how dangerous paper clips can be, modelling the correct way of using them.
Tackles new tasks confidently	Counting to 100; Making big sums; Counting backwards; Counting forever	A sequence of events representing a clear progression in the way children spontaneously set up and solve increasingly more challenging mathematical tasks after being provided with enough cognitive structuring by the teacher.
Can control attention and resist distraction	Fixing a bike	A child has entered the workshop area and has decided that he is going to fix the bike that has been placed there as part of the setting. The child remains on task for an extended period of time using different tools and checking the outcomes of his actions.
Monitors progress and seeks help appropriately	Building a bridge	A group of children have decided to build a bridge to get to a castle but the bridge keeps falling down. The 'builders' actively seek the advice of other children that stop in front of the construction to see what is happening.
Persists in the face of difficulties	Finding the screwdriver	A girl has entered Santa's workshop area. She is looking for the screwdriver to make some toys. She actively looks for it and asks for the other children's help. After 15 minutes where she appears to have been engaged in other activities, she finally finds it: 'I found the screwdriver!'
PROSOCIAL ELEMENTS OF INDEPENDENT LEARNING		
Negotiates when and how to carry out tasks	Planning the game Playing in a small group	A group of children have been encouraged to create a game using a hoop and a ball. The children actively discuss who is going to hold the hoop and who is going to throw the ball. They all agree they have to take turns. 'Otherwise it wouldn't be fair', says one of the children. They try out the game before teaching it to the rest of the class.

Statement	Exemplar Event	Description
Can resolve social problems with peers	Negotiating the number of children	Too many children are in the workshop area. A child becomes aware of the situation and acts as a negotiator trying to determine who can stay and who has to leave. He uses different questions to solve the problem: 'Who doesn't want to be here?', 'Who's been here the longest?'
Is aware of feelings of others; helps and comforts	Making cards	A girl helps a boy make a card. She doesn't 'do' it for him but has been asked to show him what to do. During the sequence, she is very helpful and 'keeps an eye on him'. She does not take over, yet seems to take pride in the helping process.
Engages in independent cooperative activities with peers	Enacting the Three Little Pigs crisis	Children are playing Three Little Pigs in the role-play area. A 'crisis' has been introduced. The Big Bad Wolf has stopped the electricity getting to the house. The children are exploring using torches and working out what to do.
Shares and takes turns independently	Taking turns	A group of girls are playing a lottery game. They spontaneously take turns asking: 'Whose turn is it?' and reminding each other: 'It's your turn now!'
COGNITIVE ELEMENTS OF INDEPENDENT LEARNING		
Is aware of own strengths and weaknesses	Counting beans with Jack	A girl is counting beans using a puppet (Jack). Being aware that there are too many beans to count, she decides to put some of the beans away so Jack can 'count them better'.
Can speak about how they have done something or what they have learnt	Drawing a fire	Two boys sit side by side at the drawing table and discuss how to draw a fire. One says it is a zig-zag shape and draws an example, saying that his mummy told him it was like this. The other disputes this and says it goes little and then very big, drawing small downward lines and long vertical lines. They talk about how fire is spread and how the flames move.

(Continued)

(Continued)

Statement	Exemplar Event	Description
Can speak about planned activities	Setting up a castle	Two girls have decided that they want to make a castle in the play area. Being prompted by the teacher's questions, they verbalise what they want to put in the castle, the materials they need and what to do first.
Can make reasoned choices and decisions	Writing an animal story	Two boys collaborating on a story decide between them that they want it to feature a particular animal so send someone in search of a picture to copy.
Asks questions and suggests answers	Learning about skeletons	A group of children were interested in skeletons, and the nursery nurse helped them to draw around one another and copy pictures from books to fill in their skeletons. The children felt the bones in their bodies as they drew. They asked questions about the bones and in some cases one child answered another's question.
Uses a strategy previously modelled	Giving peer support in writing	Two boys support another with his writing when they see him struggle. They communicate clearly, using strategies they have heard from their teacher, and are sensitive to his feelings.
Uses language previously heard for own purposes	Writing messages	Two girls help a boy who also wants to write. They track what he is doing and point to an example of a message (written by a child) on the wall and draw attention to the individual letters, naming them for the boy.

MOTIVATIONAL ELEMENTS OF INDEPENDENT LEARNING

Initiates activities	Making computers	Two children decide to make a computer out of a cardboard box. They work collaboratively together and persist when things don't go well, for example when working out how to join the box (computer screen) to the table.

Statement	Exemplar Event	Description
Finds own resources without adult help	Recreating the story of *Goldilocks and The Three Bears*	The children have decided to recreate the story of *Goldilocks and The Three Bears*. They have found three boxes of different sizes for the beds, three bowls and spoons for the bears and a pot to cook the porridge in.
Develops own ways of carrying out tasks	Making books	One child made a 'book' by sticky-taping together three small sheets of computer paper. She drew simple illustrations and asked her teacher to scribe the story for her. It was a perfect story: 'The cat was lost. The flower was lonely. The dog had no friends. The sun came out and cheered them all up.' The book was read to the class and four weeks later, half the class had made books using the same method.
Plans own tasks, targets and goals	Wrapping Christmas presents	A group of children have turned the play area into Santa's workshop. They have decided that they are going to wrap presents; they have found resources, and they have negotiated their roles.
Enjoys solving problems and challenges	Building a bridge	The teacher has set up a challenge: the children need to get a treasure located at the other side of the room, crossing a river filled with crocodiles. The children decide to build a bridge and they cooperate to achieve their plan.

Figure 7.2 Children's Independent Learning development (CHILD) statements and exemplars

SUMMARY

In order to enhance the experience of *emotional warmth and security* for the children in your class or setting, you can:

- show an interest in the children as people, and share aspects of your own personal life
- act playfully and have fun, showing enjoyment of the children's natural playfulness
- provide a model of emotional self-regulation, talking through emotional difficulties, including your own (for example, when something happens which annoys you), with the children
- show that you appreciate effort and enthusiasm at least as much as what the children produce or achieve.

In order to enhance the experience of *feelings of control* for the children in your class or setting, you can:

- make sure that children have access to a range of materials for their own playful purposes
- give children the opportunity to make choices about activities
- discuss classroom rules and routines, the classroom layout and the provision within your setting with the children, and take on board their ideas
- involve the children in the design, development and maintenance of role-play areas, displays, etc.
- adopt a flexible approach to timetabling which allows children to pursue an activity, including playful activities to their satisfaction, avoiding unnecessary interruptions.

In order to enhance the experience of *cognitive challenge* for the children in your class or setting, you can:

- require children to plan activities
- consider whether activities planned to be carried out individually could be made more challenging as a collaborative group task
- ask genuine, open-ended questions that require higher-order thinking – why, what would happen if, what makes you say that?
- give children opportunities to organise activities themselves, avoiding too-early adult intervention.

In order to enhance the experience of *talking about their learning* for the children in your class or setting, you can:

- encourage children to play, solve problems or carry out activities in pairs or small collaborative groups
- plan for and encourage peer tutoring, where one child teaches another
- involve children in self-assessment

- make learning intentions explicit when tasks are introduced or discussed, either while the children are engaged in the task or afterwards in a review session
- model a self-commentary, which articulates thinking and strategies (for example, when making a junk model and selecting materials).

QUESTIONS FOR DISCUSSION

- Are self-regulating children always the best behaved? Why might that not be the case?
- How can we improve opportunities for the children in our setting to take control of their learning?
- Are we guided in our provision by the children's interests?
- Do we ask children metacognitive questions about their learning?
- Do we reward effort rather than products and encourage children (perhaps by modelling?) to believe they can improve through effort?

ACTIVITIES

A. Assessment through activities

There are a number of tasks which have been designed to assess particular aspects of children's self-regulatory abilities. A number of these assess children's inhibitory control, i.e. their ability to not do the obvious thing, but to deliberately do something different. This is widely recognised as a fundamental building block towards achieving cognitive and behavioural control, and develops over the early years of life, although at quite different rates in different children. Children with ADHD have poor inhibitory control. Examples of these tasks are:

1. *Simon Says*: you almost certainly know this, and there are lots of variations, such as the good pig and the bad wolf (only do what the good pig says – you need puppets for this version!); it is great fun to play with your class to wake them up, or to fill in an odd 5 minutes while you are waiting, but it also tells you a lot about children's inhibitory control.
2. *Luria's hand game*: developed by the famous Russian psychologist, it is played by an adult and a child (or two children if they like!) and simply consists of person A either making a fist or putting their hand out flat on the table; in the first part of the game, the child, or person B, simply copies whatever person A does (say for 20 goes); but in the second part of the game, they have to do the opposite. It is very revealing!
3. *Ponitz et al.'s (2008) Touch your toes task*: this is very similar to Luria's hand game, except that children are required to touch their head or touch their toes and, in the second part of the game to again reverse the rule. These simple tasks are remarkably predictive, certainly with children under 5, of general self-regulatory development.

B. Assessment by observation

The CHILD observation instrument can be used in a variety of ways. You can observe individual children on a number of separate occasions, in a range of contexts, and collect examples of where they show particular abilities related to individual statements.

I would suggest, as an exercise to begin with, that, in consultation with another member of staff who works with the same children, that you select 3 children from your class (of whom you have the general impression they might be high, medium and low in terms of ability) and both yourself and your colleague observe each of these three children for 3–5 minutes on 5–6 occasions (preferably not the same occasions) over the course of a week. You should then both make a general assessment of the children's levels of self-regulation. You should assess whether, for each statement, your observations suggest that the child is always (score 3), sometimes (score 2), occasionally (score 1) or never (score 0) capable of showing this behaviour. You can then compare the profiles of the 3 children as assessed by yourself and your colleague. Examining disagreements between yourselves will be a particularly productive exercise in developing your shared understandings of the meanings of each of the statements, and of your assessments of each of the children.

You can then go on to use the instrument to assess other children in the class or group, perhaps particularly those about whom you have some concerns. You can repeat assessments after a few months to track development. You may also find using the instrument is a valuable audit of your provision. For example, often practitioners have said they realised they couldn't assess children's abilities to make reasoned decisions or resolve social problems or choose their own resources, because they were not given this opportunity.

References

Barkley, R.A. (1997) *ADHD and the Nature of Self-Control*. New York: Guilford Press.

Black, P. and Wiliam, D. (1998) *Inside the Black Box: Raising Standards through Classroom Assessment*. London: King's College School of Education.

Blair, C. and Razza, R.P. (2007) 'Relating effortful control, executive function, and false belief understanding to emerging math and literacy abilities in kindergarten', *Child Development*, 78, 647–63.

Blöte, A.W., Resing, W.C., Mazer, P. and Van Noort, D.A. (1999) 'Young children's organizational strategies on a same–different task: a microgenetic study and a training study', *Journal of Experimental Child Psychology*, 74, 21–43.

Bronson, M. (2000) *Self-regulation in Early Childhood*. New York: Guilford Press.

De Corte, E., Verschaffel, L. and Op't Eynde, P. (2000) 'Self-regulation: a characteristic and a goal of mathematical education', in M. Boekarts, P.R. Pintrich and M. Zeidner (eds) *Handbook of Self-Regulation*. San Diego, CA: Academic Press.

Deloache, J.S., Sugarman, S. and Brown, A.L. (1985) 'The development of error-correction strategies in young children's manipulative play', *Child Development*, 56, 125–37.

Dignath, C., Buettner, G. and Langfeldt, H-P. (2008) 'How can primary school students learn self-regulated learning strategies most effectively? A meta-analysis of self-regulation training programmes', *Educational Research Review*, 3, 101–29.

Fabricius, W.V. and Hagen, J.W. (1984) 'Use of causal attributions about recall performance to assess metamemory and predict strategic memory behaviour in young children', *Developmental Psychology*, 20, 975–87.

Flavell, J.H., Beach, D.R. and Chinsky, J.M. (1966) 'Spontaneous verbal rehearsal in a memory task as a function of age', *Child Development*, 37, 283–99.

Forman, E.A. and Cazden, C.B. (1985) 'Exploring Vygotskian perspectives in education: the cognitive value of peer interaction', in J.V. Wertsch (ed.) *Culture, Communication and Cognition: Vygotskian Perspectives*. Cambridge: Cambridge University Press.

Goleman, D. (1995) *Emotional Intelligence*. New York: Bantam Books.

Istomina, Z.M. (1975) 'The development of voluntary memory in preschool-age children', *Soviet Psychology*, 13, 5–64.

Leat, D. and Lin, M. (2003) 'Developing a pedagogy of metacognition and transfer: some signposts for the generation and use of knowledge and the creation of research partnerships', *British Educational Research Journal*, 29(3), 383–416.

Maki, R.H. and McGuire, M.J. (2002) 'Metacognition for text: findings and implications for education', in T.J. Perfect and B.L. Schwartz (eds) *Applied Metacognition*. Cambridge: Cambridge University Press.

Meyer, D. and Turner, J.C. (2002) 'Using instructional discourse analysis to study scaffolding of student self-regulation', *Educational Psychologist,* 37, 17–25.

Nelson, T.O and Narens, L. (1990) 'Metamemory: a theoretical framework and new findings', in G. Bower (ed.) *The Psychology of Learning and Motivation: Advances in Research and Theory, Vol. 26*. New York: Academic Press.

Palincsar, A.S. and Brown, A.L. (1984) 'Reciprocal teaching of comprehension-fostering and comprehension-monitoring activities', *Cognition and Instruction,* 1, 117–75.

Paris, S.G. and Paris, A.H. (2001) 'Classroom applications of research on self-regulated learning', *Educational Psychologist,* 36, 89–101.

Pekrun, R., Goetz, T., Titz, W. and Perry, R. (2002) 'Academic emotions in students' self-regulated learning and achievement: a program of qualitative and quantitative research', *Educational Psychologist*, 37, 91–105.

Perry, N. (1998) 'Young children's self-regulated learning and contexts that support it', *Journal of Educational Psychology*, 90(4), 715–29.

Perry, N., Vandekamp, K.O., Mercer, L.K. and Nordby, C.J. (2002) 'Investigating teacher–student interactions that foster self-regulated learning', *Educational Psychologist,* 37, 5–15.

Pintrich, P.R. (2000) 'The role of goal orientation in self-regulated learning', in M. Boekaerts, P. R. Pintrich and M. Zeidner (eds) *Handbook of Self-Regulation.* San Diego, CA: Academic Press.

Pintrich, P.R. and De Groot, E.V. (1990) 'Motivational and self-regulated learning components of classroom academic performance', *Journal of Educational Psychology,* 82, 33–40.

Ponitz, C.E.C., McClelland, M.M., Jewkes, A.M., Connor, C.M., Farris C.L. and Morrison, F.J. (2008) 'Touch your toes! Developing a direct measure of behavioural regulation in early childhood', *Early Childhood Research Quarterly*, 23, 141–58.

Reder, L.M. (ed.) (1996) *Implicit Memory and Metacognition*. Mahwah, NJ: Lawrence Erlbaum.

Sangster Jokic, C. and Whitebread, D. (2011) 'The role of self-regulatory and metacognitive competence in the motor performance difficulties of children with developmental coordination disorder: a theoretical and empirical review', *Educational Psychology Review,* 23, 75–98.

Schaffer, H.R. (2004) 'The child as apprentice: Vygotsky's theory of socio-cognitive development', in *Introducing Child Psychology*. Oxford: Blackwell.

Schunk, D.H. and Zimmerman, B.J. (eds) (2008*) Motivation and Self-Regulated Learning*: *Theory, Research, and Applications*. Mahwah, NJ: Lawrence Erlbaum.

Siegler, R.S. (2002) 'Microgenetic studies of self-explanation', in N. Granott and J. Parziole (eds) *Microdevelopment: Transition Processes in Development and Learning.* Cambridge: Cambridge University Press.

Sugden, D. (1989) 'Skill generalization and children with learning difficulties', in D. Sugden, (ed.) *Cognitive Approaches in Special Education.* London: Falmer Press.

Veenman, M., Wilhelm, P. and Beishuizen, J.J. (2004) 'The relation between intellectual and metacognative skills from a development perspective', *Learning and Instruction,* 14, 89–109.

Wang, M.C., Haertel, G.D. and Walberg, H.J. (1990) 'What influences learning? A content analysis of review literature', *Journal of Educational Research*, 84, 30–43.

Whitebread, D. (1999) 'Interactions between children's metacognitive processes, working memory, choice of strategies and performance during problem-solving', *European Journal of Psychology of Education*, 14(4), 489–507.

Whitebread, D., Anderson, H., Coltman, P., Page, C., Pino Pasternak, D. and Mehta, S. (2005) 'Developing independent learning in the early years', *Education 3–13*, 33, 40–50.

Whitebread, D., Bingham, S., Grau, V., Pino Pasternak, D. and Sangster, C. (2007) 'Development of metacognition and self-regulated learning in young children: the role of collaborative and peer-assisted learning', *Journal of Cognitive Education and Psychology*, 6, 433–55.

Whitebread, D. with Dawkins, R., Bingham, S., Aguda, A. and Hemming, K. (2008) 'Organising the early years classroom to encourage independent learning', in D. Whitebread and P. Coltman (eds) (2008) *Teaching and Learning in the Early Years,* 3rd edn. London: Routledge.

Whitebread, D., Coltman, P., Pino Pasternak, D., Sangster, C., Grau, V., Bingham, S., Almeqdad, Q. and Demetriou, D. (2009) 'The development of two observational tools for assessing metacognition and self-regulated learning in young children', *Metacognition and Learning*, 4(1), 63–85.

Index

Added to a page number 'f' denotes a figure.

WORKING MEMORY AND LEARNING

A Practical Guide for Teachers

Susan E Gathercole *University of York* and
Tracy Packiam Alloway *University of Stirling*

Dr Tracy Alloway has been awarded the prestigious Joseph Lister Award from the British Science Association.

'The authors have written a guide for practitioners that is both highly practical, and yet based upon sound theoretical principles. This book achieves a successful, yet often elusive, link between theory, research and practice, and deserves to have a high readership. I will have no hesitation in recommending it to a range of readers'
- Jane Mott, Support for Learning

A good working memory is crucial to becoming a successful learner, yet there is very little material available in an easy-to-use format that explains the concept and offers practitioners ways to support children with poor working memory in the classroom. This book provides a coherent overview of the role played by working memory in learning during the school years, and uses theory to inform good practice. Topics covered include:

- the link between working memory skills and key areas of learning (such as literacy & numeracy)
- the relationship between working memory and children with developmental disorders
- assessment of children for working memory deficits
- strategies for supporting working memory in under-performing children

This accessible guide will help SENCOs, teachers, teaching assistants, speech and language therapists and educational psychologists to understand and address working memory in their setting.

2008 • 144 pages
Cloth (978-1-4129-3612-5) • £66.00
Paper (978-1-4129-3613-2) • £21.99
Electronic (978-1-4462-0038-4) • £66.00

ALSO FROM SAGE

IMPROVING WORKING MEMORY

Supporting Students' Learning

Tracy Packiam Alloway *University of Stirling*

By developing and improving a child's working memory, you will see improvements in their achievements at school, and in their concentration. Better working memory can be particularly useful to children with conditions where poor working memory is thought to be an underlying factor.

Such conditions include:
- dyslexia
- dyscalculia
- speech and language difficulties
- developmental coordination disorders (motor dyspraxia)
- ADHD (attention deficit hyperactivity disorder)
- autistic spectrum disorders

This book explains how to spot problems early, and how to work with children to improve their working memory, therefore increasing their chances of success in the classroom. It is packed full of practical strategies to use with students, but it also explains the theory behind these activities.

Underpinned by rigorous research and written in a highly accessible style, this book will appeal to practitioners, parents and students as an essential guide to helping their students fulfil their maximum potential.

2010 • 136 pages
Cloth (978-1-84920-747-8) • £65.00
Paper (978-1-84920-748-5) • £21.99
Electronic (978-1-4462-4796-9) • £65.00

ALSO FROM SAGE

PLAY AND LEARNING IN THE EARLY YEARS

From Research to Practice

Edited by **Pat Broadhead** *Leeds Metropolitan University*, **Justine Howard** *University of Swansea* and **Elizabeth Wood** *University of Exeter*

Providing high quality play experiences is an essential part of good early years education, but this can pose a challenge for practitioners who face pressure from a more didactic primary curriculum, and from parents worried that their children will fail to acquire essential skills and knowledge.

By helping the reader to develop their understanding of the complex relationships between play and learning, this book examines current theoretical perspectives on play, alongside examples of recent and innovative play research from a range of disciplinary and methodological perspectives. With contributions from leading play scholars, it brings together theory, research, policy and practice in relation to play and learning in early years settings. The emphasis is on the relationship between play and learning, and play and pedagogy, and the need to understand these dimensions more substantially in order to teach with confidence.

There are chapter objectives, reflective points, reflective tasks and suggestions for further reading throughout, to facilitate critical thinking and encourage independent study. Suitable for early years practitioners, early childhood students at undergraduate and postgraduate levels, and all those who work with and care for young children, this is an exciting and thought-provoking book.

2010 • 208 pages
Cloth (978-1-84920-005-9) • £68.00
Paper (978-1-84920-006-6) • £21.99
Electronic (978-0-85702-703-0) • £68.00

ALSO FROM SAGE

LEARNING IN EARLY CHILDHOOD

A Whole Child Approach from birth to 8

Edited by **Pat Beckley** *Bishop Grosseteste University College*

By explaining the theoretical context and highlighting relevant research evidence, this book supports a whole child approach to learning in the early years. Drawing on case studies from a wide range of early years settings, the chapters consider how the different professions in education, health and social care can work together to achieve the best possible outcomes for all young children.

The links made between theory and practice, and the practical suggestions for how to make this happen in any early years setting, make this book a vital text for all early years students.

November 2011 • 264 pages
Cloth (978-1-84920-404-0) • £65.00
Paper (978-1-84920-405-7) • £21.99

ALSO FROM SAGE